INsourcing Innovation

INsourcing Innovation:

How to transform business as usual into business as exceptional

Defining a roadmap for STRUCTURED INNOVATION
using the Theory of Inventive Problem Solving (TRIZ)

David Silverstein   Neil DeCarlo   Michael Slocum

BREAKTHROUGH
PERFORMANCE PRESS

Longmont, CO

Breakthrough Performance Press
2101 Ken Pratt Blvd Suite 201
Longmont, CO 80501

ORDERING INFORMATION

Quantity Sales: Discounts are available for quantity purchases by resellers, corporations, institutions, associations, and others. For details, contact 303-684-5888, or visit www.insourcinginnovation.com.

Individual Sales: Contact 303-684-5888, or visit www.insourcinginnovation.com.

Library of Congress Control Number: 2005906821

ISBN: 0-9769010-0-5

10 9 8 7 6 5 4 3 2

Acknowledgments

As with any major undertaking, the completion of this book was the result of many people's dedication, intelligence, and hard work. We owe a debt of gratitude to them all, and we want to recognize them for their irreplaceable contributions.

First, we acknowledge the father of TRIZ, Genrich Altshuller, who recognized a long time ago that it's easiest to achieve creative breakthroughs with a roadmap. We pay our respects to the late Mr. Altshuller, because he not only had the rare foresight to see this, but he also had the unstoppable passion to assemble the underlying body of research that led to the validation of innovation's code.

We also acknowledge the hundreds of TRIZ practitioners who helped Altshuller fulfill his dream, and who have applied his principles and practices with great success. The stories of their accomplishments are told in these pages, and the companies for which they work are mentioned too. Many of these are clients of ours, and we readily acknowledge that their work is the real work of innovation. As we teach them how to implement TRIZ, we learn from them every bit and more than we teach.

We thank our development and copy editor, Tere Stouffer, for her incredible professionalism and her uncanny ability to keep us on track — not to mention her laser skill and tenacity. Without Tere, this book would be much less than it is. We're also indebted to our colleagues at HWH Public Relations, Wendi Tush and Cassel Kroll, who helped us get out of the mire of our own thoughts when it was necessary.

No book would be complete, or readable, without its tables and figures, and without a good overall visual design. Eve Vrla created the cover of *Insourcing Innovation*, as well as many of the figures inside. Colin Moore also created many figures in the book, and he did all the page design and production work. It was obvious that Colin and Eve cared about our book as much as we did, and that was invaluable to us.

Additionally, we would like to acknowledge Wendy St.Clair, Scott McAllister, Jodee Bennett, Kimberley Carrington, Renée Roberts, and David Lampo for their input and proofreading, along with Mary Kidd for her work in indexing the book.

Table of Contents

Foreword

by Dr. Mikel Harry

Circumstances in business don't often come together to create the opportunity for radical change. Yet today, we sit on the precipice of just such an opportunity; we peer over the edge and see that a process for innovation is surely evolving. Of course, one of the key tools that fuels this process is TRIZ.

TRIZ is a methodology like Six Sigma. It has grown and developed in response to a very difficult and critical business requirement: the need for constant reinvention and continual innovation. For a business to be successful, it needs to constantly and consistently improve what it does —in a never-ending, world-class manner. But it also needs to innovate in a never-ending, world-class manner.

We all know the story behind business quality in America and in the world. For as much activity and resources that companies poured into ensuring quality, something was missing. The United States got its wake-up call when it lost market share in several key industries. When it investigated the cause, it found a drastically different culture and approach at companies like Toyota.

Today businesses talk a lot about innovation, and about how certain foreign countries are better at innovation than we are. I even hear and read a lot about structured innovation, and about "innovation methodologies." Yet I don't hear anything very specific. There is no Toyota Production System for innovation. There is no Lean for innovation. There is no viable approach and roadmap that people are debating.

Although TRIZ is known and used by many, it is not commonly recognized by all. Yet when I look over innovation's edge, that's what I see. I see in TRIZ a method much like Six Sigma was before it became institutionalized: an extremely powerful approach to meeting a critical business need that's cloaked in a little mystery and a modicum of fear. I see in TRIZ a methodology like DMAIC that is greatly worthy of debate.

TRIZ comes across as "technical" to many, because the books that have been published about it to date have been oriented to the mind of the pure inventor. Until *Insourcing Innovation*, no book about TRIZ has articulated its use and value in terms everyone can understand.

I want every business leader to read this book, because it contains a message they need to hear: What at first seems technical, scientific, and esoteric has the power to transform a corporation. Also, I want every scientist and engineer to read this book, because it will challenge them to make the act of innovation more commonplace and effortless.

The essence of Six Sigma and its key role has been to transform organizations from a preoccupation with the business of quality to a system for improving the quality of business. Although the former is driven from the mindset of narrow vision and firefighting, the latter is a function of an audacious view that a company can be consumed with quality in everything it thinks and does.

If it's strategically time for your company to reinvent itself from top to bottom, the TRIZ methodology can greatly facilitate this drive. Like what Six Sigma did for quality, TRIZ can enable the transition from the business of innovation to the innovation of business. I am proud to be associated with and to endorse the authors of *Insourcing Innovation*. I believe their message is one that every business leader should hear.

Preface

We wrote this book because most business leaders are dissatisfied with the ability of their companies to innovate. Companies consistently pour money into R&D, yet inconsistently achieve their innovation objectives. In fact, no other aspect of business is as frustrating and out of control as innovation. At the same time, innovation is core and central to business success.

This is the paradox we address in *Insourcing Innovation*: so much touting of the need for breakthrough, yet so little knowledge about how it happens. The paradox exists because most people who are responsible for innovation are simply too smart for their own good. With all their experience, they still struggle to generate high quality, high density, and high velocity breakthroughs.

TRIZ, the Theory of Inventive Problem Solving, is a necessary supplement to the power of your company's best minds. It doesn't replace the need for smart people, just as a method like Six Sigma doesn't replace that need. But like Six Sigma, TRIZ comes into play as a structured system for accomplishing objectives the best people can't accomplish — no matter how many you have in your company or how smart they are.

Thought leaders, CEOs, consultants, and scientists alike are calling for innovation that's more measurable, reliable, predictable, streamlined, and effective — in essence, better and faster. The answers to the call range from appointing an innovation leader to establishing a better innovation process. Some have called for a better alignment of all innovation success factors: people, process, leadership, creativity, culture, investment. Others have suggested various programs to follow, most, if not all, of which consist of a certain set of principles and guidelines. As innovation experts, we have our own such set, and you discover more about it in this book.

But mostly what you get in this book is a hardened methodology for making innovation more manageable, controllable, and profitable. For every dollar you spend on innovation, you want a dollar back, and a whole lot more. You want to safeguard and optimize your investment in innovation, and the best way to do this is to make it as turnkey as possible. Our book discusses why most of the so-called "methods" are really just guided brainstorming sessions that don't get inventors out of their own mental boxes, even though they claim to do so.

This is why most current methods fail. They're grounded in psychological inertia and divergent thinking. The TRIZ methodology asserts that every innovation objective has a finite set of possible solutions, given constraints. The way to discover these solutions is to converge on them quickly and reliably through a universal pathway everyone can learn and understand. Why not teach your brightest and best how to travel this pathway, and why not have them teach it to others?

This is the central theme of our book: The way to increase your company's innovation value proposition is to take control of it yourself, not to outsource it. Although there are potential benefits to outsourcing innovation for some companies under the best circumstances, we don't accept this view as viable in the long-term picture of business. Innovation, like quality improvement, is a skill you want as many people as possible to master.

Lest we be cavalier, this is not a new idea. Innovation expert Gary Hamel has said that there are tools, processes, and systems for driving innovation that almost anyone can learn. Hamel has called for a "mobilization and monetization of the imagination of every employee" in the style of how Toyota realized a positive ROI by investing in the problem-solving skills of every employee.

Basically, innovation isn't and shouldn't be a sometimes thing, driven by the bright few and held back by the average many. Rather, innovation should be an all-the-time thing driven by trained people in every part of the organization. With such collective momentum, an organization breaks the stronghold of its own inertia and creates a true force of continuous evolution.

Specifically, *Insourcing Innovation* is organized into the following four parts:

- Part One provides a simple framework for thinking about business excellence, a historical viewpoint of management thinking and practice, a rationale for implementing structured innovation, and the case for why TRIZ is a world-class method for achieving perpetual innovation with existing resources.

- Part Two covers the tactical aspects of TRIZ, with a central focus on the TRIZ methodology (DMASI) and its primary constructs, techniques, and components. Part Two also provides several implementation case examples, including an in-depth breakdown of how TRIZ was used to create an innovative self-heating beverage container.

- Part Three transitions from the tactical to the strategic aspects of structured innovation (TRIZ), which show you that no single innovation can stand alone. All tap into one or more of eight evolutionary forces to become what they are. Part Three describes these forces along with related anecdotes and examples.

- Part Four discusses how structured innovation is part of the larger system of "total performance excellence." It shows how other key aspects of business excellence enable structured innovation, and at the same time are enabled by structured innovation. Part Four looks at these aspects and shows how they're related.

Clearly, it's time to shine more light on the path of innovation — to define it and call it out, unequivocally, like the Yellow Brick Road. Perhaps business leaders have enough innovation hindsight and need more innovation foresight. Maybe it's time to make structured innovation a core competency and quit the habit of noticing how much sense innovation makes . . . after it happens.

Part One:

Interrupting Innovation Inertia

Why the Theory of Inventive Problem Solving (TRIZ)
has the power to transform

"There are no strategies for creating wealth in the long term that are not driven by innovation."

—Gary Hamel

1
Winning the Innovation Race

The act of innovation is an act of conceiving the future, which is what great companies do. They give birth to new ideas that, when commercialized, improve the quality of life for their customers and themselves. This is why we don't fault any executive or manager for passionately embracing innovation as a critical business success factor.

At the highest level, the capital available for innovation can be the difference between *business as usual* and *business as exceptional*. We define "business as usual" as performing just well enough to stay alive or make a small profit. "Business as exceptional," on the other hand, is the state a company achieves when it enjoys greater profit margins by virtue of greater innovation.

Exceptional companies, in turn, invest a portion of their good profits into driving successive waves of innovation. Like a snowball effect, greater net profitability for each innovation, and more innovations, drive what we can characterize as the dream of every business to become a consistent cash machine through changing times.

Management guru Peter Drucker once said that innovation is the only competitive advantage a company really has, because quality improvements and price reductions can be replicated, as can technology. Therefore, if a company could have just one major capability, it should be innovation. In his book, *Managing for the Future*, Drucker makes two related points: 1) Every new product, process, or service begins to become obsolete on the day it breaks even and 2) Making your own products, processes, or services obsolete is the only way to prevent your competitor from doing so.[1]

Creative destruction. Planned obsolescence. Making something new under the sun. Call it what you want — every business alive should be making its own wares, as well as its competitors' wares, obsolete. There's not a CEO who would disagree, because they all know that innovative companies enjoy greater growth and success.

But despite almost excessive lip service to the importance of innovation, there are a few curious questions. Why, if innovation is so critical, do so few have a process for teaching it to people? Why do fewer rather than many understand how innovation really happens? Why do so few measure and manage innovation to their own satisfaction?

In *Innovation 2005*, the Boston Consulting Group (BCG) reported the results of a global survey on innovation. From a group of 940 executives,

74 percent said that their companies planned to spend more on innovation. Yet fewer than half of these said they were satisfied with their historical return on innovation spending.[2]

The call of this report is like the call of so many others. Find a way to get more out of your innovation investment. Shorten the time between innovation development and innovation commercialization (the concept-to-cash cycle). Develop a culture of people who innovate freely and effectively. Bring the proportion of innovations attempted to innovations made much closer to 100 percent. Most important of all, measure the process and outputs of innovation better. (See Appendix 1, The Economics of Innovation.)

The central theme of this book is that all the current calls for innovation lead to one place: the need for a world-class methodology that can bring all the elements of innovation success together. We believe and argue that TRIZ (short for Teoriya Resheniya Izobretatelskikh Zadatch in Russian) is that methodology, because it's the only approach that enables a corporation to concertedly and productively converge on the right innovative solutions, in all areas of what it means to be a business.

We spend a lot of time throughout this book showing you why this is true. For now, we make the simple observation that much of the thinking, literature, and practice of innovation is in a free-form state. While there are many different approaches to facilitating the innovation process, none is globally considered to be the most rigorous, reliable, replicable, and scientific one.

Business leaders have scientific methodologies for improving performance and solving problems, but they don't have an analogous methodology for improving innovation. What you do have is a belief that innovation is an act of creation, not systemization, and that's why innovative capability can't be programmed into an organization the way, say, quality improvement methods are. Or at least that's the predominant thinking and practice in business today.

Allow us to make an analogy of sports cars, which are fast, beautiful, exotic, and, of course, designed to win races. For many years, Ferrari and Lamborghini were accepted as the fastest and most furious super-cars money could buy. But all that changed around the time Acura came out with the NSX, a sports car that could do what the other high-end machines could do, but at a much lower price tag. Additionally, and more importantly, the Acura was built with consistent high reliability and quality compared to its Italian counterparts.[3]

The exotic Italian super-cars enjoyed their run as marginally reliable machines until Acura raised the standard. V12 power and superior styling were not enough anymore. After all their years of success, the Italians had to reinvent themselves, which they did after about a decade of reluctant improvements to the way they build their fanciest cars.

Fast forward a couple of decades and the story gets more interesting. Recently, according to *USA Today,* Acura put the kibosh on the NSX because of various issues with emissions and safety regulations. Even more significant, Acura and others now make cars that are as "powerful and sophisticated" as the NSX, but that can be bought for a fraction of the NSX's $90,000 price tag. That which revolutionized the sports car market (NSX) has been out-revolutionized by newcomers and advancing innovation. This is the story of innovation, as it creates a wave that is outdone by another wave, and another wave, and so on.

Today there is an interesting phenomenon in the world of innovation practice that we can liken to the advent of the affordable and reliable sports car. The current cadre of innovation thought leaders are generally comparable to the Ferrari and Lamborghini sports cars of the 1960s, 1970s, and even the 1980s. They have best-selling books, prestigious professorships, and enviable centers for processing research and serving corporate clients. They are fast and furious.

Large, already-successful companies with money to spend hire these innovation gurus to help them evolve strategically, and the result of that relationship is then analyzed and presented to the public in the form of journal articles and books. When business executives then read about the success of Wal-Mart or Cisco or Dell, relative to others in their respective industries, they interpret that to mean these gurus can certainly help them to become more innovative.

At a minimum, they believe these gurus to have the inside track on how the various market leaders became market leaders, and maybe they hire them to tell as many secrets as they possibly can within some standard of ethics. No, we're not saying that the current cast of innovation thought leaders don't have the utmost integrity; nor are we saying that their contributions are not important. The affordable, reliable sports car would not be what it is today without the heritage and influence of its less reliable, fast, stylish, and expensive precursors.

All we're saying is that it's time to raise the bar of innovation to one that is more repeatable, teachable, deployable, manageable, and reliable. Just because very intelligent people can make observations and see a trend — and can describe this trend in a book or article — does not mean they have a system for making innovations plentiful and commonplace. In fact, the aura of innovation is still one of rarified air. Innovation isn't common, stupid; that's why it's called *innovation*.

Although this thinking seems to make perfect sense, and although it resonates with big executives who hire big innovation gurus, the thinking is flawed. The lack of an innovation Acura is more a function of complacency than of natural constraint. Unusual business success has always been a function of uncommon sense, not of common sense as many would argue, and if common sense says innovation has to be rare, then it's wrong.

TRIZ is the Acura of innovation relative to the Ferraris and Lamborghinis. It is the answer to the evident lack of quality and reliability in the way most companies go about reinventing themselves. Fortunately, TRIZ is here, and systematic innovation is possible. With TRIZ, companies have a way of improving innovation acumen, and they also have a way to make innovation more reliable, predictable, and pervasive.

Continuing on the topic of race cars, they have to perform three functions to be successful. One, they have to accelerate. Two, they have to brake. Three, they have to corner. If a car has any chance of winning, it has to perform all three of these functions better than the others do.

Yet as important as these functions are, what underlies them? What is the most basic and crucial aspect of winning a race? Yes it is the perfect coordination of accelerating, braking, and cornering that wins the race, and all the systems and components of a car converge on these three aspects of success. But there is something more fundamental, and that is the ability of each tire to grip the road. It is the coordinated, optimized traction of four patches of rubber as they meet the road that determines how well a car can accelerate, brake, and corner to win a race.

It is this same traction a company seeks when it sets out to make innovation common and reliable. This is the high-level formula by which a company transitions from common sense to uncommon sense when it comes to innovation. This is the point of differentiation between conducting business as usual and conducting business as exceptional.

For a corporation, the four patches where the innovation rubber meets the road are culture, infrastructure, methodology, and proficiency. Culture is the ability to shape innovative behavior and practices on a widespread scale. Infrastructure is the technology and management supports that are necessary to grow and reinforce innovation. Methodology is the standard roadmap for implementing innovation projects with a high probability of payoff. Proficiency is the ability to ramp up world-class innovation capability in the shortest possible amount of time.

Together, these four cornerstones form the critical success factors of innovation ROI. As with race cars, each of these factors needs to be coordinated and balanced according to the demands of the day. To be agile, to stop or slow when necessary, to speed up around a hair-pin turn, a race car must distribute power between its four wheels to maximize grip. Similarly, a corporation must constantly distribute power among the four elements of innovation to maximize ROI.

If any one element is missing or isn't coordinated with the other elements under changing circumstances, the results are undesirable. At a minimum, the car loses the race and the corporation loses opportunity and money. At a maximum, the car spins out of control, flips over, crashes into a wall, and causes a fiery demise for itself and maybe even its driver. The same is true for a corporation.

Ideally, innovation is an all-wheel-drive activity, with constant activity and load distribution around culture, infrastructure, methodology, and proficiency. Although the current state of thought leadership addresses many aspects of all-wheel-drive success, some elements are lacking. TRIZ fills those gaps and brings us to a time when innovation is much more than cool and notable, like a Ferrari. TRIZ ushers us into an age when innovation is also reliable and accessible, like an Acura, while not losing its cool.

With all-wheel-drive innovation, an organization allocates human capital, financial capital, and technological resources in a coordinated way so it can maintain traction while accelerating, braking, and cornering at high speeds. This is the ultimate goal of systematic innovation: Run the course of business better and faster than your competitors so you win the bigger prize.

To do this, of course, you have to see the road ahead. Race car drivers always know the course in all its detail so they are not surprised by unexpected changes. That's great you say, for racers, but businesses don't always have a good visualization of the course with all its unexpected twists and turns. True, but the good news is that systematic innovation, or TRIZ, provides a much better view of the course than what a business would see without it.

Imagine sitting at street level in Pasadena, California anticipating the start of the Rose Bowl parade. You can see the floats come around the corner, but only one at a time. You don't know how many there are, how fast each is moving, or where the last float is. All you can do is react to the pace and progression of what's coming at you. This is the way most organizations approach innovation. They sit at street level and try to figure out what the market is doing by observing visible trends.

But what if you were in a helicopter? How much parade would you see then? You would see the first float, the last float, and every float in between. You would know how fast each float is moving, when each stops and slows, and even when the parade will end. Like the race car driver who knows every detail of the course ahead. Like the organization that takes itself out of the innovation Ferrari and puts itself into the innovation Acura. Like the TRIZ practitioner who flies not by the seat of his pants but by the horsepower and lift of an innovation flying machine.

You see throughout this book why and how TRIZ enables you to see the road ahead, to be agile and accurate in your R&D endeavors, and to provide traction to your innovation drive on all four accounts of culture, infrastructure, methodology, and proficiency. Ultimately, this will ensure better performance and sustainable economic viability. Taken to its full extent, systematic innovation enables a corporation to create the future, which, according to Peter Drucker, is the best way to predict it.

2
Evolution of a Big Idea

From a bird's eye view, we can define business holistically as the ongoing act of creation and improvement. (See Figure 2-1.) You create something new to offer to customers, and then you try to make it better (improve) while also trying to come up with something new or different again (innovate). In an overarching sense, this is how businesses evolve: as a function of the healthy tension and fine line between innovation and improvement.

What business should know today about innovation is what it knew about improvement a long time ago: There is one answer, just one answer, to every problem, if you can only find it! Leaders like Deming, Juran, and Crosby forged the pathways of what it means to take quality

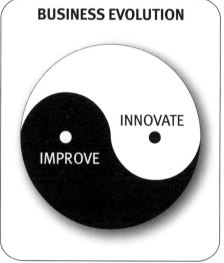

BUSINESS EVOLUTION

INNOVATE

IMPROVE

2-1: Business is the cyclical interplay of innovation and improvement. An organization creates something new, improves it, and then makes it obsolete by creating something new again.

seriously and personally, to believe it in your heart and to live it with your initiatives. Because of this major shift, almost all corporations employ the tools of quality with great conviction, and those who don't are stuck in the Dark Ages of business.

Yet the other half of the business equation, innovation, is still mired in ambiguity and lack of structure. Evolution hasn't yet carried the mass of modern business to a place where it can agree on what constitutes world-class innovation practice. And there surely isn't a roadmap, common language, or set of standards that can be effortlessly exchanged between companies, suppliers, partners, executives, managers, engineers, employees, functions, departments, and the rest.

In the world today, you're either good at innovation or you're not, and your goodness or badness isn't a function of how well you follow a standard roadmap, because there is none.

Or at least there isn't one that a tipping-point full of organizations understand. Sure, you have innovative companies that drive themselves by organic growth. A good example is Proctor & Gamble, which has done very well in increasing revenues over time without too many acquisitions. When P&G does acquire, it wants companies that have their own organic innovation engine in place. In a CNBC interview, Gillette CEO Jim Kilts said that one of the biggest reasons for P&G's bid to buy Gillette was its innovation in men's grooming products and batteries.[4]

Whirlpool is another example of a company moving fast toward systematic innovation. When you think about an industry like appliances, it's readily apparent that there is "a sea of white products with little to differentiate them except price." These are the words of Dave Binkley, Whirlpool's senior vice president of global human resources.[5]

About five years ago, former Whirlpool CEO Dave Whitwam saw a vision of a company obsessed with innovation, because he saw this as a lacking competency. Today, there are a lot of people at Whirlpool working to make innovation commonplace, and the company believes it can train anyone to innovate.

Says Whirlpool VP of Corporate Planning and Development Harry Burritt: "In the 1980s, the [watchword] was quality; today, it's innovation . . . But the two are not mutually exclusive . . . Now we want superior quality and faster cost reduction, plus innovation — all at once."[6]

It's clear that most have developed the skill of improvement very well with all its tools, methodologies, roadmaps, and quantified results. But only the rare few are driving headlong like Whirlpool toward making innovation an embedded and core competency. Even when companies profess a commitment to innovation, they struggle to materialize that call.

In a global survey of 175 companies by communications consultancy Hill & Knowlton, executives cited "promoting continuous innovation" as the most difficult goal for their company to get right. "Structurally, many companies just aren't set up to deliver continuous innovation."[7]

Echoing this, PricewaterhouseCoopers conducted a survey that asked nearly 1,000 CEOs what levers they thought were most important in driving revenue growth. Forty percent of them said that "innovation" and "unique products and services" are most important, while only four percent said IT and the Internet were the most important.

What does this tell you? It tells you that the ability to systematically innovate in general is much more important than the ability to optimize any one particular innovative wave, such as the Internet. It tells you, simply, that you'd better be good at innovation if you want to be good at business.

Authors Mark Epstein, Robert Shelton, and Tony Davila wrote a book released in 2005 called *Making Innovation Work: How to Manage It, Measure It, and Profit from It.* "Many times, companies look at innovation as something that requires a level of creativity that they are not used to dealing with, something unbounded," Epstein says. "They are afraid if they bound it, they will kill whatever creativity might have been fostered."[8]

Epstein, a visiting professor at Harvard, continues to characterize what he and his co-authors learned after talking with CEOs and conducting surveys: "We found in our research that to harness creativity and innovation and use it to develop new products, you need a structure of processes and measures."[9] The processes to which Epstein refers are mostly grounded in better measurement and reward systems. Ideally, these systems are dovetailed with a methodology like TRIZ.

American Executive magazine wrote an article called "The Science of Invention," which was based on the work of Epstein, Shelton, and Davila. One of the subtitles of the article was "rampant incrementalism," and this strikes us as an accurate characterization of modern business culture. Although the improvement side of the business equation is replete with structures and tools (ISO 9000, Baldrige, Six Sigma, TQM, Continuous Improvement, etc.), the innovation side is lacking systems and structures.

Here again, the authors of *Making Innovation Work* are instructive. "People get so focused on incremental innovation that they starve the semi-radical or radical innovation that could provide them really big benefits," says Shelton. "They just get locked into little changes and never look at the other part of the portfolio."[10]

The key for business is that improvement and innovation are elements of a balanced whole, and if they are out of balance, overall sustainability and profitability will suffer. You need enough improvement-type projects running in parallel with more aggressive innovation projects, such that the more predictable income from the former funds and fuels the latter on an ongoing basis. By doing this, a company ambidextrously fulfills its obligation to both elements of business success (improvement/innovation).

Yet it's perplexingly clear that for all the talk about innovation, and the need for balance between invention and improvement, there is no widely known, proven, standard methodology. Where are the tools, methods, roadmaps, and quantified results of innovative adaptation? of planned obsolescence? of creative destruction? Many business leaders like to talk about innovation, but don't plan it, deploy it, manage it, measure it, and track it in the same way as improvement is planned and measured. Most business leaders don't champion innovation like improvement, don't live it the way improvement is lived. Yet it's critical to the survival of an organization.

We mention in Section 1 that the premise of this book is the lack of a widely known, proven, and standard methodology for structuring innovation in today's corporations. We also mention that TRIZ holds the key to what companies want regarding innovation: system, structure, method, control, predictability, measurability, and return on investment. In Part Two of this book, we detail the TRIZ methodology and highlight some companies that are implementing TRIZ with success.

But before we do this, it's important to take a short detour onto the path of how management methods develop over time. When we have a snapshot of how key management methods start, mature, and become institutionalized, we have the proper perspective of TRIZ in its historical context. With this perspective, it's also much easier to understand why TRIZ is so important before delving into the details of how it works.

Every institutionalized management method follows a similar S-curve progression, starting out as a *good idea* and ending up as a *big idea*. (See Figure 2-2.) By this, we mean that a methodology is first applied by companies slowly and sporadically across the full spectrum of the global economy and its various sectors. Then the methodology passes through a number of milestones before becoming institutionalized as a household practice for the majority of organizations across the world.

At first, a good management idea resonates with a handful of people in a localized environment. This initial impulse then slowly but steadily gains acceptance and popularity, usually amongst those in the scientific community. After this, there is a period when early adopters pioneer the application of the concept in a pilot environment. If the forming methodology has traction, meaning that it works, a groundswell of organizations build microcosmic capability around it. The principle is proved in a localized way, which clears the way for applying the new system in a much more pervasive way.

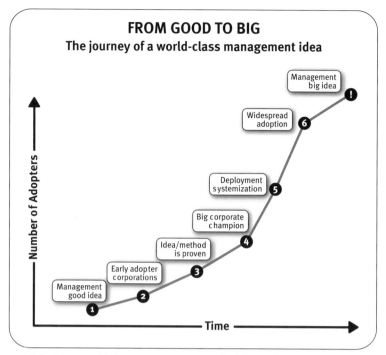

FROM GOOD TO BIG
The journey of a world-class management idea

2-2: Every world-class management methodology of the past century has followed a common life path with common milestones. TRIZ is no exception to the rule.

After this the destiny of a methodology depends upon a small group of influential business leaders, or one business icon like Jack Welch (in the case of Six Sigma). When certain executives in certain companies start touting a methodology as the new way, a lifepath inflection is made, and the methodology is adopted at a steeply increasing rate.

The next critical step on the path from good to big is the convergence of the methodology with a proven value proposition at the corporate level, not just at the local level. This is when the methodology has been deployed throughout many organizations, and its operational formulas have been standardized and documented. We call this *deployment systemization*, because the ROI of the new way can be realized on a widespread and repeating basis.

With all barriers to implementation removed, and with a tipping point of organizations speaking the same language, the next big management idea is locked into history. After a decade or some period of time, after many companies have synthesized their experience and best practices, the system is perfected and institutionalized into a world-class methodology. This is the abbreviated version of how certain methodologies become widely known, accepted, and practiced.

In the words of two authors who examined 50 management big ideas of the past several decades: "In examining these 'Big Ideas' of the past few decades, it is hard to say that many were *totally* new when introduced. In fact, many were based on case studies of companies already practicing some form of them. But it was the synthesizing and systemization that was new."[11]

Therefore, the business world has the institutionalization of many ideas and methodologies, such as ISO 9000, Six Sigma, Reengineering, Management by Objectives, TQM, Voice of the Customer, Strategic Planning, Customer Relationship Management, Benchmarking, and others. And if you travel further back in time, you could include such other methods as Scientific Management, Statistical Process Control, Quality Circles, the Toyota Production System, and others.

Inasmuch as each management big idea was formed by its own progressive S-curve events, they themselves are the events that form even larger management S-curves. Of course, each management big idea is also comprised of several smaller components. TQM, for instance, embodies such elements as the Voice of the Customer, Empowerment, Teambuilding, and Continuous Improvement. TRIZ is an umbrella for Substance-Field Modeling, the 40 Inventive Principles, the Eight Evolutionary Patterns, and so on.

3
Structured Innovation is Here

Look at Figure 3-1 and notice that we've highlighted three very important S-curve progressions in the evolution of business management: Productivity, Quality, and Innovation. You can study these successive macro waves to demonstrate why Structured Innovation is the new source of competitive advantage.

As much as we have selectively picked and chosen a few names and companies to represent much larger phenomena, we readily acknowledge the popularized nature of the choosing. No it wasn't just Taylor, Ford, Ohno, Toyota, and Womack that made the act of productivity optimization a reality. It was thousands of people and companies. And no, it wasn't just Deming, Juran, Hammer, Harry, all the Baldrige Award winners, and GE that made quality improvement the mature force it is today. The only way an S-curve becomes an S-curve is at the behest of the many, not the few.

Given this cursory and stylized view, the first major wave of management focus was Productivity, which was the emphasis at the time of mass

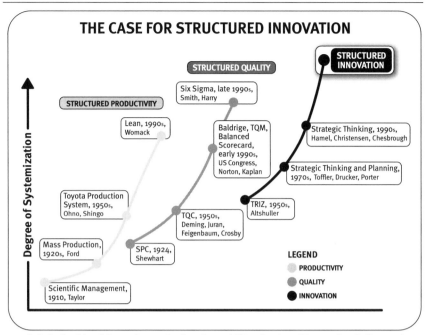

3-1: In the big picture of organizational capability, structured innovation is the next frontier for development and systemization.

production with the pioneering work of Fredrick Taylor's time-and-motion principles. Then, first with Ford in a rudimentary way, and later in the 1950s with Toyota, the systemization of productivity had reached a major inflection point on the S-curve. Finally, in the 1980s and 1990s, after several decades of conceptual and methodological evolution, the practice of waste and time reduction (productivity) became consolidated under one big, proven, turnkey umbrella called Lean.[12]

The second wave was Quality, which began with Walter Shewhart around the same time that Fredrick Taylor's productivity-oriented time-and-motion principles became hardwired into the way companies did business. As it goes with evolution, about the time one focus is gathering momentum another focus is born. Making a lot of poor quality products in a short period of time with fewer resources could only take a company so far on the competitive landscape. In hindsight, it seems obvious and natural: After companies figured out how to make a lot of products in a short period of time, the next frontier was to increase the quality of those products.

With the help of agents like Dr. Edwards Deming, the Japanese led the way in shifting the baseline of world-class business. After the principle of TQM was proved, and after a critical mass of companies adopted its sound practices, quality became a necessary prerequisite for competing on the global field. We can say that today, Six Sigma has solidified the drive for quality into its most mature form.

Third came the wave of systematic Innovation, which began with the work of Genrich Altshuller in 1946. Here was a Russian scientist who refused to believe that the act of generating a patent was one of creative genius. He said:

> Although people who had achieved a great deal in science and technology talked of the inscrutability of creativity, I was not convinced and disbelieved them immediately and without argument. Why should everything but creativity be open to scrutiny? What kind of process can this be which unlike all others is not subject to control? . . . What can be more alluring than the discovery of the nature of talented thought and converting this thinking from occasional and fleeting flashes into a powerful and controllable fire of knowledge.[13]

We wonder from where Altshuller might have borrowed his opinion, or from what consciousness it arose. Could it be that the fire of systemization would only naturally spread from the tree of productivity to the tree of quality to the tree of innovation? Surely Altshuller asked the right question: "Why should everything but creativity be open to scrutiny?" Thus, the field and practice known as TRIZ began to grow and proliferate.

As you saw in Figure 3-1, on the Innovation curve, the call and methods of strategic innovation took center stage in the 1970s, and again in the 1990s, with Peter Drucker, Gary Hamel, and the rest. But that's not what's interesting. What's interesting is that the lineage of Innovation has a disconnect between its tactical and strategic paths, and this has caused the terrible dichotomy that lies at the root of why so many talk about innovation yet so few do it well.

Hang on while we explain. For decades, TRIZ has been applied to the extremely challenging technical barriers facing those who actually have to design and make new products — the hard part of any call for innovation. At the same time, the strategic innovation thinkers have challenged the status quo with their stories and analogies of how certain principles and practices from one industry can be migrated into another — or how any business can change its model, by virtue of creative adaptation, in order to break out and achieve new success.

We won't bore you with the rehashed stories of Wal-Mart, Dell, Microsoft, and the others, like IBM, which couldn't for the life of itself see the obvious trend toward the PC. The key about all these stories and those who tell them is that they have created a mass innovation consciousness that believes something very dangerous. The strategic innovation thought leaders have made everyone believe that innovation is a product of great minds thinking analogously, openly, creatively, and compellingly.

Yet the fact is that all strategic and technical innovations fall in line with various patterns, parameters, and principles — all of which are contained in the body of TRIZ knowledge, and in this book. Although this body of knowledge is oriented toward making innovations through *constructively convergent thinking*, almost all current methods are oriented to making innovations through *destructively divergent thinking*. The former is fast and reliable, while the latter is relatively time consuming and unreliable.

The trick and truth is that there's a place for both types of creativity in the drive for constant innovation. A company needs the divergent methods of creativity, and it needs the convergent process of TRIZ, depending on the specific strategic or tactical tasks at hand. What companies don't need anymore is pep talks and spending that simply throws money at the people or companies believed to have what it takes to knock down the innovation wall. As the title of our book implies, companies need hard innovation capability that they can own, proliferate, manage, and control.

The main problem, which we highlight more in Part Two, is that businesses have much more bias toward psychologically inert methods of creativity than they do toward scientifically sound methods of breakthrough. We explain in more detail why the former methods tend to be divergently destructive, while TRIZ is convergently constructive.

We're not trying to discredit the enormous contributions of Michael Porter, Gary Hamel, Clayton Christensen, and the many others in industry who have used the power of brainstorming, open analogical thought, and individual strategic brilliance to bring about structural change in business. Their thought leadership and practice have resulted in many cash cows. We're just saying that the success of innovation to date, on a historical timeline, is more like the culture of the Wild West than of industrial society, and it's time for innovation to evolve.

4

The Further Rise of TRIZ

Now we can look again at the S-curve framework for how a good management idea, or methodology, becomes a big one adopted by nearly all and practiced by so many. Note in Figure 4-1 the thick line that represents the trajectory of TRIZ, still in the stage of slower proliferation among early adopter companies. Although dozens of companies have significant

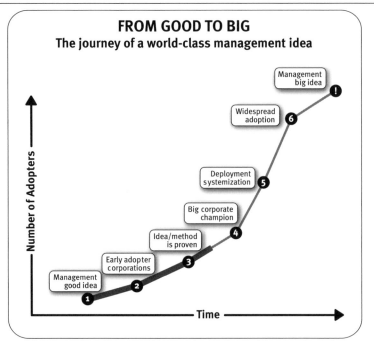

FROM GOOD TO BIG
The journey of a world-class management idea

Number of Adopters →

Time →

- ① Management good idea
- ② Early adopter corporations
- ③ Idea/method is proven
- ④ Big corporate champion
- ⑤ Deployment systemization
- ⑥ Widespread adoption
- ! Management big idea

4-1: Every world-class management methodology of the past century has followed a common life path with common milestones. The path of TRIZ is represented by the heavier line that is approaching its first major inflection point.

experience with TRIZ, hundreds more have staff who either know about TRIZ or practice it in some informal, minimal, or ad hoc way.

With such a groundswell, and the evolutionary precedent that all major business drives eventually become embodied by a methodology, TRIZ is poised to become the de facto standard for tactical innovation (products and services). As well, the eight evolutionary patterns of TRIZ covered in Part Three are robust enough to become the de facto standard for strategic innovation.

Although the envelope of innovation is larger than TRIZ, businesses are converging on TRIZ for innovation the way they have converged on Lean and Six Sigma for operational excellence. Although Lean and Six Sigma are not the only approaches, they embody all the best principles and practices for improving operations. TRIZ is not the only approach to structured innovation, but it embodies the best of what all such methods try to achieve.

Stepping back in history for just a moment, in the early days of mass production, companies approached quality improvement the way business approaches innovation today: as a special task for special people. At that time (early 1900s), the big differentiating business drive was volume, and almost everyone in company operations was focused on metrics of productivity, or the number of units produced over time, regardless of their quality. When quality issues arose, highly skilled and educated people would solve them if they could. Only very few people knew how to plan for quality, improve quality, and solve quality problems.

As the mass economy grew, however, more variation and defects occurred, and this spawned the need for more and better quality control. Quality, therefore, not volume, became the new differentiator, so companies went quality crazy. They launched initiatives, developed tools, standardized processes, solved problems, collated customer requirements, issued philosophies, institutionalized roadmaps, trained people, measured defects, and praised those who embodied the quality imperative. By necessity, quality became everyone's job, not just the job of a few.

As it tends to do, the proverbial wave of change took what was once uncommon knowledge and made it common to all. More organizational force was exerted to improve quality in every operation, every process, every job — because the competitive imperative to do so demanded this, and because the cost of poor quality was too high. In the same way, today the cost of poor innovation is too high, and the innovation imperative is eclipsing the quality imperative.

Therefore, more companies are poised to gain competitive advantage by making innovation more systematic and structured. You see it in autos, and you certainly see it in electronics: Basic quality is implied, and the differentiating drive is to develop new models and variations with increasing speed, functionality, and value.

These industries, in fact all industries, although differentiated along the lines of quality, are greatly differentiated by their ability to provide new styling, options, features, and lifestyle choices. People buy from Toyota and Sony because of their reputation for quality. But they also buy from these companies because they perpetually innovate and provide the next coolest thing.

In 2004, the Harvard Business School press published a series of articles on innovation written by various authors and pulled together by thought leader Clayton Christensen. As a whole, the articles tell an interesting story about the circumstances under which innovation happens. In the introduction of the series, Christensen says that there is a roadmap for improving the ability to create growth through innovation. First, you identify prospective opportunities. Second, you assess the potential for selected opportunities. Third, you begin the iterative process of execution.[14]

These three points are the organizing outline for about a dozen of the best articles on the subject — all of which provide high-level advice for proceeding toward the goal of strategic breakthrough. One article, for example, provides a framework for evaluating winning product breakthroughs along the lines of "lower price," "easy to use," "easy to buy," and "greater benefits."[15] The closer a product comes to satisfying all of these dimensions, the closer that product comes to fulfilling the goal of disruptive change.

But the overwhelming question, and the one that begged us to write this book, is how? How to innovate, how to lower price, how to make easier to use and buy, how to add benefits? For all the research conducted, work done, and analyses performed by the popular innovation voices, the mass of what's available to the public is anecdotal and cursory. Current innovation constructs are high-level dictates, frameworks, quadrants and categories that lack the scientific rigor of other methodologies that exist for other purposes (productivity, quality).

It's really interesting that a world-class methodology for innovation is curiously absent from the common business mind, as is a value proposition for deploying that methodology pervasively. Although the idea of innovation is big, the practice of innovation is still relatively small. To the credit of Christensen and company, he calls for *incumbents* (market leaders) to earn their disruptive Black Belts by "developing the capability to capitalize on disruptive trends." He says, "Incumbents that have nurtured this capability could respond to a disruptive threat by setting up a separate organization or using an established process to parry the disruptive attacker."[16]

TRIZ is that established process, and the historical pattern seems clear. Given its heritage and power, it's not difficult to predict that TRIZ will continue its proliferation and become the nameplate under which structured innovation finds world-class expression. Although it's robust enough to solve any possible innovation problem at the technical level, TRIZ is also robust enough to fuel the innovation imperative at the strategic level. In short, TRIZ provides a standard roadmap and common language for all scientists and engineers in all fields, and for all business leaders in all industries.

So this begs another form of our question, how to innovate? Why has the global business community converged on a finite set of productivity and quality methods but is still regressed when it comes to innovation? If you're a CEO, you take this question very seriously for several reasons. One, innovation drives growth and profitability. Two, most companies don't have a systematic innovation engine. Three, if you build innovation capability *inside* your organization, you have a great competitive advantage, especially if you already execute quality and performance improvements on a systematic basis.

Part One: Interrupting Innovation Inertia

Business as Usual Versus Business as Exceptional

Business as Usual	Business as Exceptional
No method for innovating	Systematic method for innovating
No method for teaching innovation	Replicable method for teaching innovation
Focus on productivity and quality improvements	Focus on innovation
Forced obsolescence by competition	Planned obsolescence (and you planned it)
Talk about innovation	Plan, deploy, manage, and measure innovation
Sporadic innovation	Continual innovation
Only inventors invent	Everyone invents
Capacity to innovate is based on internal knowledge	Capacity to innovate is based on ALL knowledge

Practical Advice

- Replace the lack of a methodology for innovation with Systematic Innovation (TRIZ).

- Adopt an open innovation philosophy and adopt TRIZ to bring you solutions for adaptation.

- Integrate systematic innovation with the other corporate competencies.

- Measure innovation and demand quantifiable results on innovation projects (cost reduction, cost avoidance, or revenue generation).

- Create an internalized and sustainable innovation deployment engine on an organization-wide basis.

- Train all employees in basic TRIZ techniques so the practice of systematic innovation becomes pervasive.

- Train innovation leaders to drive innovation, select viable innovation projects, connect innovation practice and strategy, monitor and gauge innovation progress.

- Train and prepare TRIZ masters to train, coach, mentor, and facilitate the process of innovation for practitioners.

- Train specialists to enact the TRIZ methodology, complete TRIZ projects, and realize innovation ROI.

Endnotes

1   Drucker, Peter, *Managing for the Future* (Plume, 1992), p. 281.

2   "Innovation 2005," *Senior Management Survey*, Boston Consulting Group, 2005.

3   Healy, James R., "Acura Puts Kibosh on Aging but Loved NSX," *USA Today*, July 13, 2005, www.usatoday.com/money/autos/2005-07-12-nsx-usat_x.htm.

4   *CNBC News*, January 28, 2005.

5   As quoted by Pomeroy, Ann in "Cooking Up Innovation," *HR Magazine*, November, 2004, p. 46.

6   Ibid.

7   McLannahan, Ben, *CFO Europe*, CFO.com, December 10, 2004.

8   As quoted by Rose, Jill in "The Science of Innovation," A*merican Executive*, July, 2005, p. 7.

9   Ibid.

10   Ibid.

11   See Mahoney, Richard J. and McCue, Joseph A., "Insights from Business Strategy and Management "Big Ideas" of the Past Three Decades: Are They Fads or Enablers?" *The CEO Series*, Center for the Study of American Business, Washington University, January 1999.

12   Reader beware. We summarize greatly here to make a point. There were many more milestones and developments in Lean's life path than the ones we've cited.

13   Altshuller, Genrich, *Creativity as an Exact Science* (New York, Gordon and Breach, 1988).

14   Christensen, Clayton and Anthony, Scott, *Innovation Handbook: A Road Map to Disruptive Growth* (Harvard Business School Publishing, 2004), p. 15.

15   Mankin, Eric, "Can You Spot the Sure Winner?" *Innovation Handbook: A Road Map to Disruptive Growth* (Harvard Business School Publishing, 2004), p. 4.

16   Christensen, Clayton and Anthony, Scott, *Innovation Handbook: A Road Map to Disruptive Growth* (Harvard Business School Publishing, 2004), p. 45.

Part Two:

Resolving Problematic Contradictions

How the DMASI methodology, Standard Solutions, Separation Principles, Problem Parameters, and Inventive Principles of TRIZ are used to achieve tactical innovation

"Problems cannot be solved at the same level of awareness that created them."

—Albert Einstein

5
A World of TRIZ

Imagine you're the head researcher and developer at Procter & Gamble (P&G), owner of the Crest® brand and other oral-care products. Then competitor Colgate-Palmolive launches a toothpaste with whitening agents, and spawns a market that grows to $500 million in about three years time.[17] Meanwhile, sales of Crest steadily decline.

What do you do?

P&G brings in people with a reputation in other parts of P&G for instituting successful disruptive technologies, products, and solutions. "Company research at the time showed that although 50 percent of consumers wanted whiter teeth, only five percent had done anything about it."[18] The rules of teeth care were changing, and P&G had to respond. The ultimate solution came in the form of the Whitestrips® product, which, about a year after its introduction generated $200 million in revenue and close to 90 percent market share.[19]

Great, but how did it happen? The scientists on the whitening project figured the best way to compete with Colgate was to change the paradigm of applying whitener with a brush. Great again, but to do so they needed a way to make hydrogen peroxide gel stick to teeth longer than it would during a brushing cycle. And that's when they turned to another part of P&G outside the oral care area.

In its food-wrap labs, P&G had a clear adhesive film that was made into narrow strips of whitening gel that could be attached to teeth. Presto, problem solved, and without the negative consequences of tray-based whitening methods that tended to cause irritation due to overexposure of hydrogen peroxide to gums. In other words, Whitestrips are a more exacting method of sticking the whitening agent to teeth, and only to teeth.

In a 2004 article in *Strategy & Innovation*, P&G chemical engineer Paul Sagel said, "We would have hit upon the idea of a film barrier anyway, but the work the company had already done gave us a great head start. The dimpling technology developed in the food-wrap research enabled the strips to retain the gel so it stayed in longer contact with the teeth. And it gave a better in-mouth experience than a flat film."[20]

This was great for P&G, but the reality is that most organizations and companies don't enjoy the benefits of cross-industry scientific knowledge. They are not as large and diversified as P&G. And even if they are, how still do they posit that technologies in one domain will apply to another? In this case, the P&G scientists used TRIZ to solve the very difficult technical challenges behind the Whitestrips product.

We've mentioned that TRIZ is a Russian acronym that, when translated into English, is the "Theory of Inventive Problem Solving." For such a proven methodology, the name belies itself. TRIZ is not so much a theory as it is a world-class practice used by some of the world's most innovative corporations. Some of these include Procter & Gamble, Boeing, Siemens, 3M, Hewlett-Packard, Eli Lilly, Honeywell, NASA, Toyota, Intel, Johnson & Johnson, Motorola, and many others.

As pervasively as TRIZ is used across a wide spectrum of industries and organizations, it is still a relatively undiscovered methodology. Part of this is due to its abstract nature, even though that's what gives TRIZ its innovative problem-solving power. The other part is that the aggregate of business has not quite reached the place on the S-curve where it has embraced innovation as a systematic drive — although it's close and some companies are leading the way.

We've also had feedback from several client companies that TRIZ is more powerful than popular today because the brightest minds — the ones to whom organizations entrust the job of innovation — sometimes find it difficult to accept that there is a universal template for innovation. Admitting this would be to admit that the greatness of their personal minds, constantly reinforced as such since grade school, is inferior compared with the collected greatness of all inventive minds throughout history.

The more TRIZ is used to overcome complex innovation barriers, and the more business leaders become aware of its power, the closer corporations get to deploying and implementing TRIZ pervasively, like they implement any number of other initiatives. One packaged goods company trained 2,000 people in the use of TRIZ. Five years later, it increased patent

Some Companies Using TRIZ

• Avon	• Johnson & Johnson
• BMW	• Kimberly-Clark
• Boeing	• Kodak
• Borden	• LG
• Case	• Lockheed Martin
• Caterpillar	• McDonnell Douglas
• Clorox	• Motorola
• Cummins	• NASA
• Daimler-Chrysler	• NEC Electronics
• Datacard	• Pfizer
• Delphi	• Pilkington
• Dial	• Procter & Gamble
• DuPont	• PSA Peugeot Glacio
• Electrolux	• Raytheon
• Eli Lilly	• Rockwell
• Ford	• Rolls Royce
• Fujitsu	• Samsung
• General Motors	• Sanyo
• Heidelberg	• Sara Lee
• Hitachi	• Shell
• Honeywell	• Siemens
• HP	• The Gillette Co.
• IBM	• Toyota
• Intel	• USPO
• ITT	• Xerox

production by 300 percent, establishing new consumer demand categories and capturing market share from entrenched competitors.[21] For this company, improved R&D productivity is a function of structure, discipline, and rigor in the innovation engine.

The Samsung Advanced Institute of Technology recently recognized the work of its TRIZ team, whose innovations saved $91.2 million.[22] Other companies too have embraced TRIZ-like approaches to innovation, calling them an assortment of names, like "structured innovative thinking" or "systematic innovation." In the main, these various approaches are overshadowing the typical rhetoric about innovation with deployable and applicable methodologies.

In one case, a circuit board manufacturer used the TRIZ process to come up with a new surface mounting technology that eliminated field failures, saving $9 million in the first year. In doing so, the company relied on the TRIZ inventive principle of "spheriodality." (See Appendix 4 for details.) Another TRIZ project at a steel manufacturer avoided $20 million in expense by reconfiguring lot production, using several of the TRIZ separation principles.

Interestingly, TRIZ was used at the senior management level of a data security company to create a burning platform for change, resulting in the successful implementation of a performance-improvement initiative that saved $25 million in one year. Although, in this particular case, a tactically oriented TRIZ solution was found, most often strategic business leaders use one of the eight TRIZ evolutionary patterns to configure a multigenerational product plan. The specifics of tactical TRIZ are covered in Part Two, and the specifics of strategic TRIZ are covered in Part Three.

Further, Ballard Power Systems used TRIZ to innovate a more efficient fuel cell device that resulted in a 25 percent reduction in operating efficiency for a total of $11 million in savings for users. Historically and commonly, fuel cells must maintain water drainage to preserve their ability to provide power. But during extended periods of operation, they become saturated with water, and their drainage channels become ineffective at water removal.

Some Projects Where TRIZ Has Been Used

- International Space Station
- Self-heating container
- Trident missile
- SeaWolf submarine
- Cassini satellite
- Prius hybrid car
- Heat dissipation of Intel chips
- Intel board assemblies
- Lockheed Launch Vehicle
- Pluto Fast Flyby
- Delta Launch Vehicle
- Fuel Cells
- Sutures
- Blood unit tracking
- Disk drive research
- Self-heating chafing systems
- Ration heating for soldiers

In TRIZ terminology, the challenge for Ballard in making a better fuel cell resided in a specific technical contradiction. The engineers wanted to remove water from the cell, but at saturation the water channels didn't allow water to be removed. So how to redesign the cell such that water can be removed even at saturation? After going through the TRIZ process, Ballard converged on the inventive principle of "asymmetry" to solve the problem. (See Appendix 4 for details.)

Perhaps you've heard of Sterno® in a can. It's a system for keeping food or anything else hot by burning a compound of denatured alcohol, water, and gel. Before the compound contained gel, it was in liquid form, and it posed a hazard in that the liquid could spill and bring fire with it. To make the product safer and more controllable, the gel was added, which constituted a linear extension of the basic Sterno technology.

But Sterno needed a discontinuous alternative to its classic can, so it designed a heat pouch with TRIZ called the Sterno Flameless™ Heat System. It does the same job the can does, only the heat source is contained in a foil pouch that is activated by pulling a strap. With this heating system, there is no need for a match or lighter, and there is no heating flame, either exposed or unexposed to users. Says Sterno's marketing literature about the invention: "[It's] The world's first self-contained food heating system that allows you to take hot food where you never could before."

Because we describe these breakthroughs at such a high level of detail, it may seem that they could have been achieved with basic scientific knowledge, but we assure you they were not. As so many innovators know, the job of making breakthrough products and processes is anything but easy, even given all their expert knowledge. After using TRIZ, many come to have an important epiphany: It's not easy to cross the bridge from what you know to what you don't know, and this is what is required to innovate.

In Section 14, we take you on a deeper journey of how TRIZ works as applied to the technology involved in a self-heating container that was touted in *Fortune* magazine as one of the 25 best innovations of the year in 2005. We describe in some detail just a few of more than 400 technical problems that were solved with TRIZ. With this information, you can get a deeper grasp of how TRIZ works and, perhaps more importantly, why it's a necessary tool for all companies to have and own.

Here's the problem we aim to fix with this book: Nearly 100 percent of all innovation methods boil down to unconstrained brainstorming and divergent creativity, driven by the erroneous belief that more ideas are better. In fact, more ideas are not better, because they only take you away from the one solution you need. The way to get to that one solution you need is to engage in *constrained brainstorming* and *convergent creativity*. This is exactly what TRIZ does: It provides the structure, process, guides, and tools necessary to shortcut your way to a viable innovation — the one, just one, you need to achieve breakthrough.

Although we introduce this thought here, we continue to expand it in this and other sections of this book. And we show you why and how TRIZ enables the most direct path from what you know and do to what you don't know and don't do — yet. This is the essential translation, the innovation transform function that is common to all inventive drives in all organizations at all times.

Analogously, companies use problem-solving tools like Six Sigma when for years they experience the same defect or variation issues, and they just can't figure them out with common sense, experience, wisdom, teamwork, and the like. They use Six Sigma when nothing else works, and while they're at it, they use Six Sigma to improve all processes at every level of difficulty across all functions.

Think of it this way. If you're a business leader and you want to teach people an improvement skill, you teach them Six Sigma, because you know this approach will work for the most difficult as well as the easiest problems. Companies like Samsung and the rest are converging on TRIZ as the universal insourcing solution when it comes to innovation. Although there are many methods, TRIZ is the best, because it contains the greatest degree of empirical science and proven performance.

6
The Enemy is Psychological Inertia

Before we launch directly into the TRIZ subject matter, it's important to come back to the concept of psychological inertia, which we defined in Part One. We made the bold claim that nearly all existing innovation methods are based on divergent thinking and methods of brainstorming that only help the mind think the best it can about what it knows. We mentioned, too, that the reason these methods are so limiting is that the nature of innovation is to discover what you don't know. Like any wide and perilous river, it's hard to cross without a bridge, and TRIZ is that bridge.

TRIZ forces the question of how well even special people with special genius and capabilities can formulate new strategies, products, and services in a way that meets the need of business to do this quickly and effectively. We know that most business leaders are dissatisfied with their ROI on innovation spending. And this fact leads us to characterize current approaches as inferior to TRIZ because they're all grounded in psychological inertia. This is true of the innovation methods as practiced by internal development teams, as well as firms to whom companies outsource their strategic and/or tactical innovation functions.

Psychological inertia is the sum of one's intellectual, emotional, academic, experiential, and other biases. No matter who you are, or what you know, your knowledge is meager compared with the rest of the world's. Yet almost all of more than 250 current methods of creative thinking are designed to facilitate the crystallization of what one already knows, not the discovery of what one doesn't know.

That's why current innovation practice is to hire the smartest and most creative people possible to fuel the pipeline of tomorrow's offerings. With these folks in the system, you optimize your chances that perhaps one of the 250 psychologically and/or emotionally based methods will be forceful enough to harvest genius. In other words, if current innovation methods are limited to the universe of knowledge held in smart people's heads, it makes good strategic sense to hire as many smart people as possible, and to reward them when they spin up something the company can sell.

This is how the mainstream innovation waters flow: toward stellar performers who file patents with fervor. These people are the legendary ones in companies like IBM, which has its 500-patent club and its 1,000-patent club. We don't understand how the inventors do what they do, or even what they do, but we definitely respect them as the landlords of our intellectual property. Yes, some do innovate in the absence of a structured process, even though more often than not their innovations are inferior to those they could have made with TRIZ.

The Venn diagram in Figure 6-1 shows the essence of all psychologically inert idea-generation methods. Note that the total innovation opportunity space is represented by the area of the big circle called Real Boundary Constraints. This is the total universe of what you know and what you don't know relative to solving your innovation problem. The other space of note is the one variously shaded in the middle, which is the intersection of all your personal biases — intellectual, emotional, experiential, and other in nature. As these biases intersect, and the more there are, the smaller the opportunity space for innovation becomes relative to the boundaries of all your biases, and especially relative to the real boundary space within which innovation can happen.

This is exactly what we mean when we talk about thinking outside the box. This shaded area is the box! It's the place you're locked into by

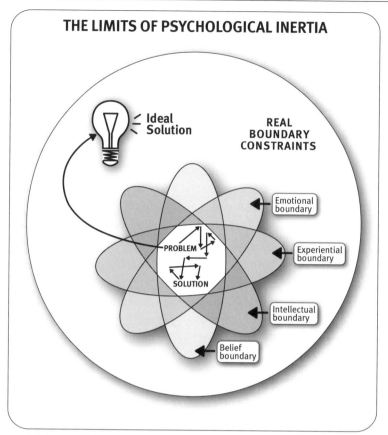

THE LIMITS OF PSYCHOLOGICAL INERTIA

6-1: Personal boundary constraints overlap to form the tiny box within which most try to "creatively" solve problems. Real creativity, and the ideal solution to an innovative problem, are much more likely to exist somewhere outside that box.

virtue of your education, past experiences, beliefs, and knowledge. It's the place of gray ambiguity, uncertainty, and doubt. Just as easily, you can think of the many intersecting biases as different people, each with their own unique bias profiles. Although approaches like the Delphi method (group of experts converging on an opinion or solution) are designed to expand problem-solving capability, often they truncate it into the lowest common denominator of what all the people involved think and believe. Although the idea and hope is that more minds yield better solutions, often groupthink rather than real breakthrough is the result.

We once held a session with 15 healthcare industry experts who were trying to come up with a new medical device. It was an impressive group of doctors, lawyers, statisticians, scientists, and engineers who had spent most of their careers in this particular area of expertise. Some in the group had multiple patents around the technology of concern, so it made sense that they were involved in finding a substantively better and cheaper way to provide the device. If any group could make a break-through, this one was it.

Anyone would have been impressed to observe this team of M.D.s, Ph.D.s, and engineers discuss and debate various ideas, all of which pointed to the idea of making a smaller device that required much less power to operate. In other words, all the discussion revolved around the "box" of making the current product smaller and/or more effective, and some very interesting ideas arose. The team converged on an idea to make a device that could run on a very small fraction of the power required to run it the current way.

But how to do this? How to create a device that could operate with 99 percent less power and, consequently, far less cost? We can't disclose the details, but we can tell you that no one had the answer until we began facilitating the TRIZ process and asking some questions about the funda-mental purpose of the device. Using TRIZ, the team generated 15 new patent disclosures in just four hours, some of which revolved around dramatic power reduction in the current system, and others around alto-gether new approaches for achieving the device's purpose.

Essentially the team defeated its psychological inertia. What would have been an exercise in continuous innovation, within the existing box of knowledge, became a journey from the known into the unknown.

Looking back at the Venn diagram in Figure 6-1, you see that the Ideal Solution to any innovation problem usually lies outside the mind of any one person or team. Therefore, when you don't use a methodological approach with the rigor of TRIZ, the probability of finding the one best solution to your problem is very, very small. As the diagram suggests, you will find a solution, but it won't likely be the *best* solution.

Without the structure of TRIZ, you're likely to meander upon a solution that is supposed to be innovative but, in reality, is only an incremental improvement over what you now have. This should be motivation enough to go inside the gray box and see what's there, because that's where the demons of innovation reside. As political and social satirist Walt Kelly once said in "Pogo," one of his famous syndicated comic strips, "We have seen the enemy and it is us."

As much of an enemy to themselves as people are, sometimes profound discovery and change do come from inside the parameters of one's own mind. Any company should acknowledge and encourage this, but never to the exclusion of taking a much more risk-free approach when possible. That said, let's examine some of the ways in which innovation classically happens before diving into the details of TRIZ.

There's the *eureka phenomenon*, whereby an innovation derives from happenstance, like when chocolate accidentally smashes into peanut butter and you get a Reese's. Like when Archimedes, the classical Greek mathematician, noticed that water became proportionately displaced when he lowered his body into a bathtub. When Archimedes discovered this, he yelled "Eureka!" while running naked through the streets of the Greek city Syracuse. People like this story, this anecdote, because it's easy to accept that this might just be how innovation occurs. You do something and witness an unexpected result, and it doesn't matter that the process isn't repeatable, because you've stumbled onto the next Big Idea.

Then there's the *enigmatic theory*, which says that certain people have a totally inexplicable yet real ability to innovate. These people live in the organizational black box, which is mostly dark and scary, even though sometimes it's an incredible source of light, principally when someone actually invents something the organization can use. One practical expression of the enigmatic world view is the market economy around hiring and retaining these mysteriously superior human beings. The organization isn't really interested in seeing how the black box works, and those who live there don't want to tell, even if they do let you peek around inside from time to time.

Another view of innovation is that it's an *unpredictable blessing*, happening when you least expect it. Sir Isaac Newton must have sat under several trees before the proverbial apple fell on his head, which then caused him to create the idea of Gravity. Again, even if this story is an anecdote, people like it because it seems like a reasonable explanation for what could be the cause of an innovation or creative breakthrough.

Yet another conception about how people innovate is by *trial and error*, which smacks so well of empiricism, which is widely perceived as a virtu-

Father of TRIZ
Genrich Altshuller (1926-1998)

Genrich Altshuller was born in Baku, Russia in 1926. By age 14, Altshuller invented a device that generated oxygen from hydrogen peroxide to aid in underwater diving. After entering a naval school in 1941 and completing the ninth grade, Altshuller was redirected by the government into a military medical school.

From there he was assigned as a patent inspector after WWII, and in 1946 he published the first article on TRIZ. Continuing his unstoppable passion for discovering the structured patterns of invention, Altshuller established a foundation for the further study of "author certificates," or patents.

About this same time, the Soviet government agreed to give the German patent library to the United States in exchange for various pieces of industrial equipment. Altshuller sharply criticized the agreement, claiming that all the equipment would be useless in 20 years, while the German patents would remain valuable.
(continued)

Incensed, Altshuller made his beliefs known by sending a letter to Stalin, with a copy to the Communist Party Central Committee and the Communist Youth Union Central Committee. This landed him a 25-year prison sentence for "anti-Soviet propaganda," but he was released in 1954, one year after Stalin's death.

While in prison, Altshuller continued the conceptual development of TRIZ and collaborated with dozens of scientists and intellectuals who were imprisoned by Stalin. His work continued over the next few decades after his release, during which time he published numerous books and articles on TRIZ, its derivative cousin ARIZ (the 76 Standard Solutions), and the Eight Patterns of Evolution.

It's only been in the last 10 years that TRIZ has become available to scientists and engineers outside of the former Soviet Union. Because of this, many inventive thinkers believe TRIZ to be in its infancy, and believe it has the potential to create a golden age of innovation even beyond that of the past 100 years.

ous scientific pursuit in the absence of any established roadmap. If you're out to break new ground, how else can you do it except by trial and error? Hold on, we'll give you the answer soon.

Because of their commonality, people understand how trial and error and other forms of psychologically inert approaches have become wired into the human psyche. After all, innovation is a one-off sort of thing; it's not something that happens every day, and it's not something everyday people make happen. Such typical thinking says that the path to new profits is made by heightened individuals who rely solely on their personal intellectual capital — the universe of what they know to the exclusion of what they don't know. The rest of this book suggests why this approach, although effective sometimes, is the biggest roadblock to remove in creating a culture of structured, continuous innovation.

7

The Mighty Russian

Before all the brilliant engineers, there were thousands of innovators, all of whom achieved great clarity of contribution as authors of registered patents. Thus there are millions of patents in countless fields of endeavor, forming an intricately connected web of patterned global evolution. If you're a business leader, you want to know what these patterns are, and you want to know what history's innovations can teach you about the ones you're trying to make now.

How can you use history's lessons as an innovation lever? What knowledge can help you springboard past the collective psychological inertia in your organization? How can you increase the scale and predictability of innovation in your company? These are questions that preoccupied the mind of a Russian engineer named Genrich Altshuller, who initiated his work in 1946, when the world was recovering from war. Altshuller's idea was that more than 90 percent of the problems faced by engineers had been solved somewhere before, beyond the natural boundaries of his mind, or anyone else's mind for that matter.

Forty years and 1,500 person-years of research later, Altshuller and others had probed into more than two million globally distributed patents and, by doing so, discovered that *innovation is not a random process*. Rather, the act of innovation is governed by set principles and follows well-worn patterns that anyone can learn. Although, at the technical level, each patent is unique, at a generic level there are really only a very finite number of problems and solutions the world over through all time! Difficult as this may seem, it's true. The millions of innovations made through time are really only a function of a very small set of parameters, principles, and patterns. The trick is to discover, and then leverage, these to meet your own innovation challenges and to engineer innovation into your DNA.

As a result of his investigative and analytical work, Altshuller and his colleagues codified eight evolutionary patterns for guiding strategic decisions, 76 standard solu-

The Tactical TRIZ Methodology

We suggest that innovation can be mapped, planned, deployed, implemented, and achieved programmatically and pervasively, and that a structured approach is not only possible but impending. The roadmap we use is DMASI (Define, Model, Abstract, Solve, Implement). Here's how it works:

DEFINE. The system and problem in question are defined and explored, and the Ideal Final Result (IFR) is formulated based on the contents of the Ideality Equation. A resource model is constructed as a reference for use throughout the DMASI process. Also, the various design challenges are framed in terms of a contradiction. Finally, a financial analysis is conducted to estimate the financial benefits expected from the project.

MODEL. The system is modeled using Function Modeling and Substance Field Modeling. The Function Model enables further understanding of how the elements in the system interact to create contradictions, or to resolve them. In many cases, technical challenges are solved at this stage with some subset of TRIZ's 76 "standard solutions."

ABSTRACT. Using abstract thought, this is when the TRIZ practitioner moves the unsolvable output of the prior two stages into the realm of the solvable. Technical contradictions are converted into generic terms per Altshuller's algorithms, then referenced to the contradiction matrix to determine applicable inventive principles. The TRIZ practitioner also uses the Abstract phase to resolve any physical contradictions with the four separation principles.

(continued)

tions for relating engineering elements in a system, 39 problem parameters for characterizing problems, 40 inventive principles for solving technical contradictions and other invention methods and tools. Together, these tools and templates form the subject matter of TRIZ.

SOLVE. The generic principles from the Abstract phase are combined with the work done in the Modeling phase to create specific solutions to the specific problem(s) under evaluation. Here, too, is where the powers of abstract thinking are important. Concept selection techniques may also be utilized to determine the ultimate feasibility of various solution pathways.

IMPLEMENT. After creating an implementation plan, the solution selected in the Solve phase is implemented so the problem is eliminated or new revenue is generated. Then the impact of the solution is compared with predicted values identified in the Define phase to confirm the demanded project ROI.

What once was the domain of only geniuses became the domain of the public, translated through a manageable taxonomy and set of methods and tools. With this taxonomy at its base, creative innovation becomes a seek-and-find mission, using the templates of Altshuller's work as guides. No longer is the ability to spawn something new a function of self-limited, open-ended methods or the happenstance of an enigmatic breakthrough.

The last thing you want to do is fashion your innovation engine solely around those with the mysterious gift of genius in the absence of a process for systematically guiding that genius. The last thing you want to do is adopt the supposition that some people have innovation mojo, while others don't. Altshuller proved that the definitive patterns of innovation can be leveraged to enlarge anyone's limited world into one of expansive possibility. In this world, the acumen for innovation isn't an inborn gift but a skill you can learn.

Maybe you've heard the story of the man who was searching under a lamppost at night for his lost keys. When a passerby asks why he keeps searching in the same place, the man replies, "Because the light's better over here." This truly is what corporations do, and Altshuller recognized this. That's why he took the rays of light coming out of everyone's individual lampposts and combined them into a bright innovation beam called TRIZ. With this light, anyone and everyone can see beyond the boundaries of their own front yards.[23]

It's hard to argue with the inherent sense of what Altshuller did, and with what has become a proven and practical collection of tools for solving complex innovation problems in a systematic way. More importantly, TRIZ is a means by which scientists and engineers — or anyone else for that matter — can move beyond their personal genius without compromising the role or value of that genius, and without subtracting the occasional value of an accidental discovery or unpredictable breakthrough. Eureka!

It's really great fun to get a eureka moment, but it's better to plan breakthroughs in a more structured way, because businesses are structured entities at their core. They establish plans, allocate budgets, measure performance, develop talent, provide forecasts to shareholders, and engage in other activities to achieve predictable profitability. Because of this, you want to make innovation more deliberate, and you're behooved to dissect its process, which is the same whether you make soda pop or rocket ships. TRIZ is that baseline you seek, because it removes all barriers and intellectual distance between those in one industry and those in another.

This is what Altshuller enabled: the use of simple algorithms to solve the most intractable problems, resolve the most difficult technical contradictions, and come up with innovative products and services. Rather than looking for answers in convenient places, TRIZ makes it convenient to find answers in difficult places.

8

Backward from Perfect

Regardless of how extensively you deploy TRIZ, or some other systematic innovation engine, one of the first steps you take is to Define your ideal state. In TRIZ, this is your Ideal Final Result (IFR), a philosophical construct that provides a measurable framework within which you can gauge progress on an innovation project, as well as an overall innovation roadmap. The IFR can also be used to create the perfect solution to strive for in problem solving.

Leonardo da Vinci has suggested that it's good practice to think of the end before the beginning, suggesting the definition of a target before taking aim. The TRIZ methodology proposes that you develop this target, so that you don't find yourself randomly shooting, and then feel surprised when you don't hit anything. From this perspective, it's not important whether the IFR is practicably attainable; what does matter is that you release the creative process from the hold of psychological inertia and accept the possibility for a perfect innovation event to occur.

The IFR is a tremendous improvement over current approaches that promote the search for mediocrity, which, of course, people refer to as "compromise." If you don't envision the IFR, you never really know how weak your resolutions are, and you never know how to gauge innovation progress. Therefore, four IFR criteria apply to the configuration of any IFR for any innovation project. One, the IFR does not introduce new harm into the system at hand. Two, the new solution preserves all advantages of the existing system. Three, the new solution eliminates the disadvantages of the existing system. Four, there is minimal or no increase in complexity.

Pragmatically, the IFR of any innovation problem is conceptualized into a metric called Ideality, which is the sum of the useful functions in a system divided by the harmful functions in a system. (See Figure 8-1.) Although the IFR is philosophical in nature, Ideality is mathematical in nature. Ideality is a useful metric, because IFR attainment is usually not possible, but multi-generational progress toward the IFR is possible and expected.

ELEMENTS OF THE IDEAL FINAL RESULT

IDEALITY EQUATION

$$\text{Ideality} = \frac{\sum F_u}{\sum (F_h + cost)} = \frac{(A_{11} + A_{22} + A_{33})}{(A_{12} + A_{13} + A_{21} + A_{23} + A_{31} + A_{32}) + cost \ (DP_1 + DP_2 + DP_3)}$$

DESIGN EQUATION

$$\begin{Bmatrix} FR_1 \\ FR_2 \\ FR_3 \end{Bmatrix} = \begin{bmatrix} A_{11} & A_{12} & A_{13} \\ A_{21} & A_{22} & A_{23} \\ A_{31} & A_{32} & A_{33} \end{bmatrix} \begin{Bmatrix} DP_1 \\ DP_2 \\ DP_3 \end{Bmatrix}$$

8-1: The Ideality Equation says that ideality is the sum of all useful functions divided by the sum of all harmful functions, plus their cost.

The A's in the Ideality Equation are derived from a Design Equation matrix, with Functional Requirements (FR) on one axis and Design Parameters on the other, in this case. The A's in the Ideality Equation represent the interactions between the FR's and DP's in the system. Of course, any domain elements of Axiomatic Design can be systemized in this way. For instance, we could make a design equation for optimizing the transformation of Customer Requirements (CR's) into Functional Requirements (FR's).

In any case, the diagonal A's in the Design Equation become the numerator in the Ideality Equation. These are the useful functions of the system (all the one-to-one correspondences on the diagonal). The non-diagonal A's are placed in the denominator of the Ideality Equation. These are the harmful functions of the system (all non-diagonal interdependencies).

In other words, concepts developed during TRIZ problem solving are not equal, and the litmus test for all innovation ideas is the metric of Ideality, which, simply stated, is the inverse of the distance between the current state of a system and the ideal state of the system. Therefore, the closer the current state is to the ideal state, the higher Ideality is.

In all, the notions of the IFR and the Ideality equation are critical in the battle against mediocrity and are, therefore, absolutely necessary ingredients of systematic innovation. If you can increase the useful functions in my system and decrease the harmful functions, with no additional cost per unit of benefit, you've achieved the objective of innovative adaptation.

It is the intention of the TRIZ practitioner to maximize Ideality by maximizing the numerator and minimizing the denominator. However, the actual calculation of Ideality may never be strictly necessary, or possible, as it's difficult to capture every element in a system, then perfectly distribute each element's impact on the numerator and the denominator — let alone normalize all the units of measure involved.

But approximations of the elements in a system and their impact on the Ideality ratio are very helpful. We, for instance, have used Axiomatic Design techniques to populate the system, depositing the diagonal elements of the axiomatic design equation into the numerator and the non-diagonal elements into the denominator, as shown in Figure 8-1.

9
All the Resources

After you've defined Ideality, you need to understand resource utilization, because you use resources to close the gap between the reality of current performance and the ideality of the optimal way. Although resource categories are common knowledge amongst value engineers, TRIZ methods focus on identifying frequently overlooked or hidden resources in a system.

To help illustrate how TRIZ helps you utilize available resources to solve a problem, or to innovate, think of a waste basket in someone's office. Inside, you have a banana peel, an empty soda bottle, several pieces of balled-up paper, a Styrofoam cup, and a plastic trash-bag liner. What can you do with these resources? How can you maximize the value you get from them? These are the questions we ask as TRIZ practitioners, and we break resources down into seven categories to facilitate the circumspect assembly of Ideality.

Depending upon what you want to achieve with your trash can, or with its contents, you can think of your resource set as constant opportunity for innovation. You have all your Substances: the banana peel, the soda bottle, and so on. You also have the generic resource of Space, which in this case could be the space between the liner and the can, the space inside the liner, the space in your cup, your soda bottle, your wadded-up paper.

How can you potentially use these resources to solve a problem or come up with a new process or application? If you look at the Field category of resources, you might utilize the chemical composition, or decomposition, of the banana peel. Maybe the magnetic properties of the trash can help, or you might be able to use the chemical properties of any soda left in the bottom of the soda bottle. How about the acoustic energy field created by filling up the trash liner with air and then popping it? You might have reason to use one of your substances in this manner.

Next is Information, like the data on the paper in the can or the contents of the soda bottle. You could derive dietary information about the trash can owner by analyzing its contents, or you could one use the soda bottle as a measuring device. If you have the information, for example the exact length of the bottle, or the diameter of its bottom, you could utilize that resource as a measuring tool.

Function is the next category, which might lead you to consider using the trash can itself as a stool, or the banana peel as a device for making someone trip, or the soda bottle to prop open a door. How you use resources all depends on your vision of Ideality and your current problem statement. Bang on the trash can to create an alarm?

Then you have Time, which could be time before the trash can gets filled, the time during which the can is getting full, and the time after it has been emptied. How is all this time utilized to optimize your objective?

The last and certainly not least resource category is People, or those who operate the system and its parts. Could the contents of the can be sorted for recycling by humans with certain skills? Could more training for people positively affect the state of the environment? Is there an ideal profile for people who perform certain jobs?

Of course, we speak here of

> ## Resource Utilization Optimization
> In TRIZ, there are seven resource categories that help you achieve Ideality and set you on the path of innovation. These resource categories are:
>
> **Substance:** Any element in a system that is substantive, such as solids, liquids, parts.
>
> **Space:** The areas inside or around a substance, such as voids.
>
> **Field:** Mechanical, electrical, thermal, chemical, electro-magnetic, and nuclear.
>
> **Information:** Data or any other information content available in a system.
>
> **Function:** What a system does, whether primarily, secondarily, inadvertently, and so on.
>
> **Time:** Elapsed before, during, and after an operation.
>
> **People:** All people involved before, during, and after an operation.

a trash can and its contents with no specific purpose in mind. But when you have a specific Ideality to increase, or problem to solve, you look for resources in each of the seven categories. When identified resources appear to be unusable, or not appropriate to your problem, that's when you couple, derive, modulate, collect, or enhance them to make them useful.

10

Build a Model, and the Rest Comes

With the Ideality equation populated, you're in a position to run scenarios for optimization, a task for various modeling techniques. Although there are many such techniques, and many that can be applied to a TRIZ-type problem or scenario, three are used most often: function modeling, substance-field modeling, and many-little-people modeling. Of course, the overall purpose of modeling is to characterize how the presence of and/or changes in certain variables affect other variables, as well as the overall operation of a system. But the real value of modeling in TRIZ is to draw out important contradictions in your system.

It's the contradictions that stump people, make you live in the paradigms of your own psychological inertia. You have to make the water cool to create a chemical reaction, but the water has to be warm to insulate the system from cold air outside. You need major mechanical leverage to execute a function, but you don't have the space in which to house a long lever. That kind of thing. This is the real essence of TRIZ: finding and solving contradictions, because they are the alchemical base of innovative transformation.

By one definition, alchemy was the medieval pursuit of taking ordinary metals and turning them into gold. Analogously, that's what you

> ### A Model's Worth a Thousand Words
>
> There are many modeling techniques used during the process of innovation, but three are most common and most powerful. They are:
>
> **Function Modeling:** A cause-and-effect model that focuses on graphically representing the problem in a manner that is conducive to the identification of contradictions inherent in the system.
>
> **Substance-Field Modeling (SFM):** The creation of triangular elements in a system that describe the field interaction between a tool and a work-piece. SFM allows for the utilization of the "76 standard solutions."
>
> **Many-Little-People Modeling (MLP):** The utilization of anthropomorphic structures to describe the functions present in a system to reveal physical contradictions in a system.

do when you innovate. You take contradictions, conundrums, and constraints, and you open them up, turn them into gold. You find ways to change the limited reality of your designs into more expansive opportunity. You perform a sort of alchemy on your processes, products, and services.

If innovation were easy, none of this would be necessary. But it isn't easy, because various useful elements in a system can also produce harmful effects in that same system. Further, it's simply difficult to get outside your own head, and industry, to even identify the contradictions that stand in the way of innovation, never mind resolve those contradictions to create order-of-magnitude change.

Standard Solutions	
Improving the system with no or little change	13
Improving the system by changing the system	23
System transitions	6
Detection and measurement	17
Strategies for simplification and improvement	17
Total:	**76**

Nevertheless, we should mention that sometimes the act of modeling will provide you with the desired solution, especially when using substance-field modeling. In other words, some systems do not present an intimidating degree of technical contradiction, so they can be optimized with less TRIZ expertise.

In such instances, further travel into the analogical process is not necessary. Instead of moving on to the Abstract phase of TRIZ (Define, Model, Abstract, Solve, Implement, or DMASI), the practitioner simply leverages one of the 76 standard solutions, all of which are based on resolving some relatively common optimization problem. See Appendix 2 for a definition of the 76 standard solutions.

11

The Basis of Analogical Thought

A 2005 *Harvard Business Review* article ("Tapping the Power of Analogy") covered the idea of how strategists think with the power of analogy. But although certain analogical reasoning can be remarkable, it can also be harmful if done poorly, say the authors. They cite the supermarket model invented in the 1930s as an analogical driver for the success of Toys "R" Us in the 1950s, and for the *kanban* system of replenishing inventory.[24] Then they cite other examples of how certain strategic analogies have failed certain companies because "it is extremely easy to reason poorly through analogies, and strategists rarely consider how to use them well."

Here's what they say:

Cognitive scientists paint a simple picture of analogical reasoning. An individual starts with a situation to be handled — the *target problem* (for Intel, the competition from makers of low-end microprocessors). The person then considers other settings that she knows well from direct or vicarious experience and, through a process of *similarity mapping*, identifies a setting that, she believes, displays similar characteristics. The setting is the *source problem* (the steel industry). From the source emerges a *candidate solution* that was or should have been adopted for the source problem (a vigorous defense of the low end). The candidate solution is then applied to the target problem.

Two points apply. First, there is no dispute that analogies are the Way of innovation. Second, the framework suggested in Figure 11-1 for achieving strategic innovation is the same as the TRIZ framework for tactical innovation. But there is one enormous difference. Although the TRIZ innovation algorithm is based on a very large amount of hard data (patent database), the algorithm suggested in Figure 11-1 is based on logic only. This is why we say that most current methods of innovation, whether strategic or tactical in nature, are person-centric; they rely on the mental powers of the individual and provide no extra help in converging on the solution needed for business or technical breakthrough.

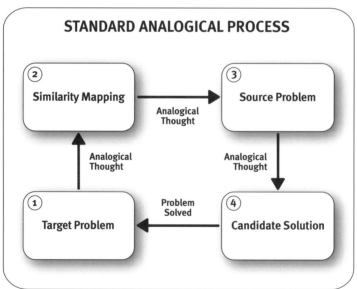

11-1: As far as current thinking goes from the most popular and pedigreed thought leaders, sound analogical thinking is required for strategic success. Such thinking also follows a certain progressive pattern, as shown above. TRIZ treats this simple framework as a springboard for greater analogical accuracy and reliability.

Although we don't want to be too critical of those who reside at the top of the Harvard innovation pyramid, we wonder why we can't find any reference to TRIZ in their work. We have observed a call for structured innovation from Harvard professor Gary Hamel, and a reference to various methodologies for making innovation learnable and doable by all. But it seems most of the other innovation leaders have somehow either missed the power of TRIZ or have overlooked it, maybe because it's still mostly a tool used by the technical community, not the executive community.

Yet the alignment is as obvious as it can be: A system of analogies rules the efficacy of innovation. The system is progressive in nature, moving always from a known problem to a known solution. In between is the tricky part, where the onus is to find the *right* analogy and manage the high *risk* of finding the wrong one. Therefore, the key is to mitigate that risk by drawing in as much convergent power as possible. Instead of diverging around an infinite number of possible solutions via unconstrained analogy, the TRIZ practitioner converges onto the right solution via structured and systematic problem solving.

Most innovation strategists believe they can reason their way to greatness with only the help of broad frameworks and models. As the authors of the *Harvard Business Review* article say about the thinking of the cognitive scientists, the strategist "identifies a setting that, *she believes* (italics ours), displays similar characteristics." Again, we don't want to be too critical, but we do want to point out that there is little place in business today for beliefs and conjectures. Science and analytics have come too far in all domains of business for anyone to rely solely on their own powers. We have databases, systems, and methods for design, operations, quality improvement, waste reduction, marketing, and so on. Yet when it comes to innovation, people seem to accept a religious rather than a rigorous approach.

Where the innovation strategists are lacking, the innovation tacticians are not, especially those who use TRIZ. This is because the body of TRIZ research, and its related analogical system, provide you with the guides and templates for making the dangerous jump from what you know to what you don't know. Using the model set up by the *Harvard Business Review* article thought leaders, we can say that TRIZ enables you to move through the analogical problem-solving process with much greater accuracy, reliability, and speed. And this is where we get very specific about how TRIZ does this, and why it can, therefore, function as an unstoppable engine for widespread innovation inside any organization.

12

Contradiction As a Path to Perfection

The gist of tactical TRIZ it is this: You start with your particular problem, or barrier to innovation. In TRIZ terms, such problems are called contradictions, which are either physical or technical in nature.[25] A physical contradiction is when one element of a system conflicts with itself, like when you need the temperature of the water to be both hot and cold to satisfy different design requirements. A technical contradiction is when two different elements of a system conflict with each other, like when you need the temperature of the water to be hot, but making it hot then interferes with some other functional requirement. In other words, as one element improves, the other degrades.

The important fork in the road is that *physical* contradictions lead you to the four separation principles of TRIZ, while *technical* contradictions lead you to the 40 inventive principles. In the case of physical contradictions, the four separation principles of Time, Space, Scale, and Condition are used to essentially divorce the bi-polarity of the element. If the water has to be hot and cold at the same time, you have to detach the water from this dilemma.[26] Either you want an element (water) to be both minimized and maximized, or you want it to exist and not exist. This is the essence of bi-polarity, and the way you resolve the contradiction is by moving through the Physical Contradiction Algorithm, as shown in Figure 12-1.

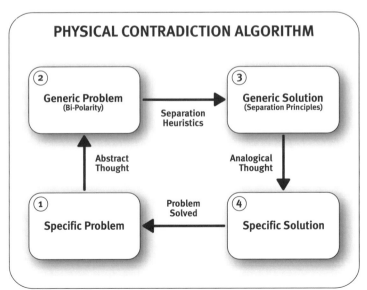

12-1: A Physical Contradiction in TRIZ is when some element of your Ideal Final Result has to be present or maximized, but also has to be absent or minimzed.

In this simplified case of the water, the TRIZ practitioner resolves the bi-polarity by applying one or more of the four separation principles of Time, Space, Scale, or Condition. Maybe the practitioner creates a Time differential for when the system needs cold water and when it needs hot water, thereby rotating its temperature according to some schedule.

Maybe she manipulates the system so it can have a separate Space for cold water and another Space for hot water, thereby enabling the conflicting needs to coexist. Whatever the physical contradiction, the goal is to resolve it by separating its contradictory requirements.

But the resolution of physical contradictions is the less complicated part of TRIZ research, although no less important. The more complex part of TRIZ research is the toolset and underlying research that enables you to resolve technical contradictions, which involve two parameters, not just one. Remember, a technical contradiction is when two elements in a system conflict with each other, and when other avenues have failed to achieve resolution.

When this is the case, the systematic innovator goes through a basic four-step process: from the specific technical contradiction elements to their corresponding generic problem parameters to certain validated generic solutions and, finally, to the specific solution(s) needed to achieve a breakthrough.[27] (See Figure 12-2.) Note the similarities and differences of this process with the one suggested by the strategically oriented algorithm displayed in Figure 11-1. While the strategist's

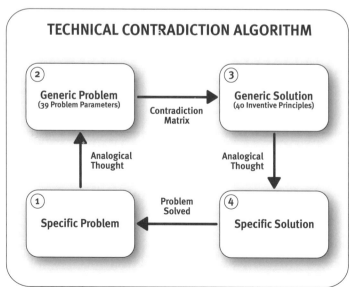

TECHNICAL CONTRADICTION ALGORITHM

(2) **Generic Problem** (39 Problem Parameters)

Contradiction Matrix

(3) **Generic Solution** (40 Inventive Principles)

Analogical Thought

Analogical Thought

(1) **Specific Problem**

Problem Solved

(4) **Specific Solution**

12-2: The heart of structured innovation is the ability to function within a simple algorithm, using the 39 Problem Parameters and the 40 Inventive Principles as tools.

approach is one of open-ended, thought-driven similarity-mapping and solution-positing, the tactical TRIZ approach converges on the one solution you need through the historically established DNA of innovation.

Let's break this process down in a little more detail before considering some real-life examples. First, the systematic innovator translates specific technical contradictions into generic terms. In other words, what is the fundamental nature of each side of the conflict? Through abstraction, the practitioner takes each specific conflicting element and finds its corresponding generic parameter. Altshuller called his generic conflicting parameters the 39 problem parameters, and they are shown to the right in summary and in Appendix 3 in more descriptive detail. Together, they represent the universe of technical contradictions that could possibly ail an engineer, or TRIZ practitioner, while trying to make some innovation or solve some problem.

For example, let's say you need more heat in a system, but that heat makes the system less safe. You have a specific technical contradiction, and you need to make it generic to get the best ideas about how to resolve it. Referencing the 39 problem parameters, you can translate the need for heat into the parameter of *temperature* (number 17), and you translate the negative impact on safety into the generalized parameter of *harmful side effects* (number 31).

Or maybe your system needs more airflow, but more airflow undesirably cools the surface. The

39 Problem Parameters

1. Weight of moving object
2. Weight of nonmoving object
3. Length of moving object
4. Length of nonmoving object
5. Area of moving object
6. Area of nonmoving object
7. Volume of moving object
8. Volume of nonmoving object
9. Speed
10. Force
11. Tension, pressure
12. Shape
13. Stability of object
14. Strength
15. Durability of moving object
16. Durability of nonmoving object
17. Temperature
18. Brightness
19. Energy spent by moving object
20. Energy spent by nonmoving object
21. Power
22. Waste of energy
23. Waste of substance
24. Loss of information
25. Waste of time
26. Amount of substance
27. Reliability
28. Accuracy of measurement
29. Accuracy of manufacturing
30. Harmful factors acting on object
31. Harmful side effects
32. Manufacturability
33. Convenience of use
34. Repairability
35. Adaptability
36. Complexity of device
37. Complexity of control
38. Level of automation
39. Productivity

need for more airflow references to general parameter number 7, *volume of a moving object*, while the cooling of the surface references to parameter number 17, *temperature.*

Classifying millions of problems into 39 categories wasn't easy for Altshuller and his team, but they did it. Then they created a contradiction matrix, by which the 39 general problem parameters are cross-referenced against themselves, yielding a total of 1,521 cells in the matrix — or 1,521 different types of contradictions. (See Appendix 5 for the complete contradiction matrix.)

Remember that a *physical* contradiction is when a problem parameter contradicts itself, and you apply any of the four principles of separation to overcome its bi-polarity. You don't use the contradiction matrix for this. But you do use the matrix to resolve any number of 1,482 different possible generic technical contradictions, the number you get when you cross-reference all of the 39 parameters with all others except themselves (1,521 − 39 = 1,482).

This was, and is, Altshuller's key contribution: He gave practitioners the ability to jump from generic problem to generic solution in one incredibly easy action. Just find the contradiction matrix cells that refer to each of your generic parameter conflicts. Inside there are numbers that refer to each of Altshuller's 40 inventive principles.

Why is this significant? Because Altshuller took all the divergent thinking strands of thousands of great minds and converged them into a sort of innovation DNA.

40 Inventive Principles

1. Segmentation
2. Taking out
3. Local quality
4. Asymmetry
5. Merging
6. Universality
7. 'Nested doll'
8. Anti-weight
9. Preliminary anti-action
10. Preliminary action
11. Beforehand cushioning
12. Equipotentiality
13. 'The other way around'
14. Spheroidality
15. Dynamics
16. Partial or excessive actions
17. Another dimension
18. Mechanical vibration
19. Periodic action
20. Continuity of useful action
21. Skipping
22. 'Blessing in disguise'
23. Feedback
24. 'Intermediary'
25. Self-service
26. Copying
27. Cheap short-living
28. Mechanics substitution
29. Pneumatics and hydraulics
30. Flexible shells and thin films
31. Porous materials
32. Color changes
33. Homogeneity
34. Discarding and recovering
35. Parameter changes
36. Phase transitions
37. Thermal expansion
38. Strong oxidants
39. Inert atmosphere
40. Composite material

He grouped hundreds of thousands of specific problems into affinity categories, and he did the same for as many of the specific solutions to those problems. This is how he came up with the 39 problem parameters and the 40 inventive principles: They are the labels he put on his affinity groupings. With this meta-data attached to the specific data, Altshuller could run analytics to discover universal, general solutions (40 principles) that are best applied to resolve certain *types* of problems (39 parameters).

All the TRIZ practitioner has to do is figure out which generalized problem parameters map to the specific technical contradictions at hand. Then the matrix yields the inventive principles others have used to solve their problems in the past, and this is how the TRIZ innovator really does stand on the shoulders of giants. When the giants are gone, their discoveries remain, and we stand on those.

Therefore, if you need the volume of the air flow to go up but the surface temperature to stay constant, what do you do? According to TRIZ, and the contradiction matrix, you go to inventive principles 2, 10, 18, and 34, because when you cross-reference the parameter of the *volume of a moving* object with the parameter of *temperature,* that's what the contradiction matrix gives you.

When you look up inventive principles 2, 10, 18, and 34, you get the following, in respective order: "taking out," "preliminary action," "mechanical vibration," and "discarding and recovering." The TRIZ innovator now has four important clues for solving the air-flow/surface-temperature contradiction.

Still, after all that, none of these inventive principles are absolutely sure to lead the practitioner to a sufficient resolution or innovative breakthrough. This is because the last step of the TRIZ algorithm is to apply analogical thinking to come up with the specific solution to the specific problem. The better an abstract thinker the practitioner is, the more likely the clues will lead to a solution.

Furthermore, there are certain instances in the contradiction matrix where no numbers appear, as you can see in Figure 12-3. This indicates that there are no data to suggest the utilization of any one or more principles over any one or more other principles. Therefore, in the instances of non-occupation, the problem-solver or TRIZ practitioner is advised to apply any or all 40 inventive principles versus any particular subset.

CONTRADICTION MATRIX CROSS SECTION

		PROBLEM PARAMETERS (39 TOTAL)		
Useful Feature	Harmful Feature	17 Temperature	20 Use of energy by standard objects	25 Loss of time
7	Volume of a moving object	2, 10, 18, 34	—	2, 6, 34, 10
14	Strength	30, 10, 40	35	29, 3, 28, 10
36	Adaptability or versatility	27, 2, 3, 35	—	35, 28

INVENTIVE PRINCIPLES (40 TOTAL)

(left side label: PROBLEM PARAMETERS (39 TOTAL))

12-3: The contradiction matrix contains Altshuller's, and many others', long and laborious research in one handy reference. This is a very small cross-section that shows the problem parameters and inventive principles associated with our stylized example (Volume of a moving object vs. Tempurature). It also shows other parameters and principles chosen at random.

13

The Power of Guided Convergence

Almost all innovation methodologies are designed to aid and expand creative thinking, so that they perpetuate psychological inertia, which is the tendency to let your own brain and heart lead the drive for innovation. The strange part is that this confounds reason, because the very thing you have to overcome when you innovate is yourself.

Spiritualists have a point of view that says you have to meditate to get in touch with your inner voice. The act of meditating itself is an act of turning off the mind and, in the space of this deactivation, the answers come through. It's your ego that keeps you from innovating! It's those voices inside your head, and all the brilliance you carry in your cadre of scientists and engineers, that keep you from receiving the answers to your innovation questions.

Here's the revelation of the counterintuitive truth: When you combine brilliant people with creative thinking tools, you get an incredible *divergence* of ideas, and this divergence makes your problem more difficult to solve, not easier. In turn, this added complexity slows your rate of innovation. The crux is to think about the nature of innovation as a *convergence* rather than divergence activity, which is counterintuitive. Intuition tells you that if you want to innovate, you need to go past boundaries, fly unfettered, explore all possibilities.

But when you think about it, innovation is really about evolutionary adaptation, and adaptation is about bringing resources to bear as efficiently as possible to resolve some specific conflict. You really don't want to diverge the problem into a thousand different streams; you simply want to converge on the one solution it needs.

Simply, when you increase the number of possible solution variants, you increase the difficulty of problem solving. The more variants you have, the more thinking, hypothesizing, and experimenting you have to do before reaching an acceptable solution, and this takes time. On the other hand, the fewer variants you have, the less trial and error you have to survive before stumbling onto the next eureka you seek.

> ### If I Had a Hammer
>
> It's true that sometimes you can use TRIZ in an abbreviated way, like you can Six Sigma. You take your tool, start chipping away at your problem, and a big chunk comes off without too much effort. Breaking that next layer off, however, can be difficult, and can require the full extent of your tool's capability.

This is a matter of simple math, and a circumspect analysis of more than 250 divergent-thinking creativity methods that essentially encourage you to spawn as many options as possible as you think outside the box. What you really want to do is converge your thinking into the right box, and then diverge your thinking within that box. Which takes you right to Altshuller's knowledge pods, his 1,482 matrix cells, the foot-springs of the organizational leapfrog.

Whatever metaphor you like, we're not unilaterally dismissing the value of psychologically based methods, like brainstorming, mind mapping, morphological analysis, Synectics, DeBono's methods, TILMAG, and all the rest. They all have their place and value, maybe especially after landing on the right pod in the contradiction matrix.

We're saying in a nutshell that innovation success is a matter of innovation horsepower, just like

> ### The Mathematical Truth
>
> Think of solving a problem in terms of $D = V/S$, where D is the difficulty of problem resolution, V is the total number of possible variants (trial and error iterations), and S is the number of possible steps that lead to acceptable solutions.
>
> Ideally, you want to make $V/S = 1$, which would mean there is only one possible variant of a solution to your problem. But we know this is rarely true, if ever.
>
> The convergent paradigm of TRIZ helps you bring your V/S ratio as close to one as possible, while the divergent nature of emotionally and psychologically based methods causes your V/S ratio to expand towards infinity.

productivity success is a matter of productivity horsepower. And we're saying that the most structured engine for improving innovation horsepower is TRIZ, the Theory of Inventive Problem Solving.

When you consider life on an organizational scale, the structure of TRIZ translates into profit by virtue of time saved and number of innovations made, because TRIZ is a repeatable process that can be easily taught, deployed, and managed. And you really have no reason to believe this isn't true, because the evolution of business is one in which formerly obscure but powerful methods become common.

14

The Case of the Containers

You may have noticed or heard about a new product called a self-heating container, made by a company called OnTech and sold under Wolfgang Puck and other brands. The container was featured by *Fortune* magazine as one of the most innovative new products of 2005. Over the next several pages, we highlight just three of more than 400 technical problems that were solved with TRIZ to make the can a market success.

As shown in Figure 14-1, by triggering an exothermic reaction inside, an OnTech beverage container safely heats its liquid content to a desirable temperature so consumers can enjoy coffee while camping, or hot chocolate at a child's soccer game on a cold day. Of course the challenge for OnTech was to make all of its containers commercially feasible, while providing the required functionality at a reasonable cost.

Here's how the OnTech container works: A button is pressed on the bottom of the can, which breaks a barrier between calcium oxide and water, which combine to create an exothermic reaction, which releases energy into the internal container, which heats the beverage that sits in an external compartment separate from the chemistry. Nothing about making an exothermic reaction is all that complicated — but making one that heats sterile beverages consistently is complicated enough to present many engineering and cost challenges.[28]

As with most all engineering challenges, you have a system to optimize, a set of objectives to meet. Customer needs are transformed into functional requirements, which are transformed into design parameters, which comprise the necessity space from which you identify system elements, both useful and harmful to your objectives. All of this is organized into a model of Ideality that maximizes the useful functions and minimizes the harmful functions, and you use various modeling and other techniques to work backward from this vision of perfection toward the best possible solution.

Innovation expert Dr. George Land of the Farside Group coined the

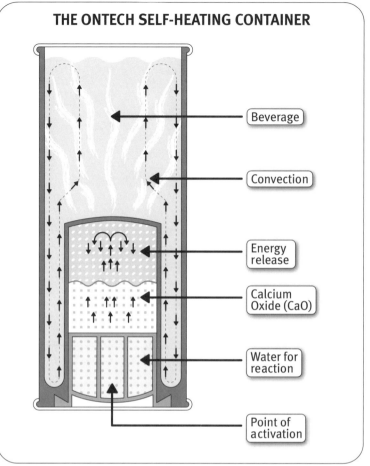

THE ONTECH SELF-HEATING CONTAINER

Beverage

Convection

Energy release

Calcium Oxide (CaO)

Water for reaction

Point of activation

14-1: OnTech used TRIZ to solve more than 400 technical problems associated with the commercialization of its self-heating container. The can's chemistry is activated by depressing a button on the bottom of the can. In a matter of minutes, the beverage in the container is heated to 140 degrees, perfect for drinking.

phrase "backward from perfect," which asserts that it's better to start with the ideal end in mind than to start from where you are and try to advance from there. This is very similar to the concept of the Ideal Final Result we introduced in Section 8, which says that the ultimate imagined outcome of the problem-solving process provides all benefit, no harm, and no cost.

The TRIZ process accepts that perfection of this sort is not attainable but, at the same time, it does not accept limitations imposed by lack of knowledge or creativity. With TRIZ, most, if not all, physical and technical contradictions can be solved, as long as you can separate the constraints of an innovation problem that are legitimate from those that are imposed by psychological inertia.

TRIZ does not accept trade-offs for contradictions where the improvement of certain functional requirements causes the deterioration of others. If this is the case, and your solutions represent compromise, you simply haven't found the best way to resolve your problem. Dr. Land says this is when you need true innovation, which he says is "an idea to resolve a problem that has not succumbed to ordinary means." That seems a fitting definition of innovation and a fitting way to describe the nature of OnTech's journey into the self-heating container. In achieving its goal of designing a can that heats its own contents, some solutions were ordinary, others less ordinary, and a couple not ordinary at all.

Work on the container project began where many TRIZ projects do: utilizing substance-field modeling, mathematical modeling, and Taguchi design of experiments to set up the basic structure of the design and to optimize several of its design parameters. One such parameter for the OnTech project was to make the outside layer of the container strong enough to resist expansion caused by the energy created during the exothermic reaction.

But after this work, several barriers to commercial viability remained, one of which was a physical contradiction related to thermal energy exposure during "retort." This is the process of heating the beverage for a set amount of time at a certain temperature to kill all pathogens and spoilagens.

The problem for OnTech was that certain materials are more able to withstand the retort process than others. As the temperature inside a container rises, as it does during retort, pressure is exerted on the walls of that container, and too much pressure will cause those walls to become misshapen or deformed. At the same time, the cooling cycle creates an internal vacuum that can distort the walls as well.

Metal, for instance, withstands retort very well. But metal is also very conductive, which means if

For the Sake of Sake

As far as we know, the self-heating can was first used in Japan for warming Sake. The drinker would poke a hole in the bottom of the can with a metal spike, which would rupture a barrier between water and calcium oxide.

The can was pretty good, but it was expensive, not recyclable, and stayed hot to the touch of the drinker. The OnTech can is cheaper, safer, potentially recyclable, not hot to the hand – and it can be molded into any proprietary shape.

you're holding it in your hand, and the beverage inside is 140 degrees, you'll probably feel it. Therefore, metal wouldn't work for the OnTech application, and the best known alternative was a form of polymer, or plastic, called polypropylene. The very top and bottom of OnTech's drinking can could be made of metal, but the sides where you hold the can had to be less conductive.

But the problem didn't end there, as it became further confounded by the fact that there are two internal chambers that are subjected to the retort process, as well as one external chamber, the outside of the can (see Figure 14-1.) Moreover, the seams that separate each of these chambers from their adjoining elements are of different natures, utilizing different materials and processes.

If too much heat resides in any chamber for too long, there is deformity and compromised integrity of function. The reason is because heat creates steam, which increases pressure. When pressure increases, it can cause various deformities in the walls of a chamber as it is built up and released. In turn, these deformities can then interfere with proper system functioning. Therefore, you need steam to do its job in the thermal warming cycle, but its job is bi-polar: It has to collapse at some time in the retort process, but it can't collapse and create unwanted deformities.

This is what you might call a conundrum, or, in TRIZ terms, a *physical contradiction*. It was definitely both for the OnTech team, which had to control the heating/cooling cycle within each of the three can chambers, while also equalizing the pressure in all chambers, generally speaking, so its device could survive the retort process.

Remember that you can address a physical contradiction, when a system element conflicts with itself, with one or more of the four separation principles (Time, Space, Scale, Condition). The OnTech team used the separation principle of Time to resolve its dilemma. By sequencing the cooling processes for each chamber at precise intervals, the strength of each successive chamber wall

> **Feeding an Army**
>
> OnTech has technology for several applications. One is the ability to heat an air-dropped, 32-pound package of food with meats, vegetables, potatoes, and desserts. Another is a self-heating tray for TV-dinner-type food.

could recover before their various pressure vacuums are maximized. Therefore, no structural deformities. Problem solved.

Still, the team had more to do in resolving two technical contradictions, the first of which was a conflict between the complexity of the materials used in the container wall and the cost of manufacturing. We've already talked about why the outside of the can had to be made of plastic, a much less conductive and less expensive material than metal — and a material that allows a manufacturer to mold the container into any number of proprietary shapes that can be trademarked.

However, this doesn't talk specifically about oxygen ingress, or the tendency for oxygen to seep through certain materials, like plastic, during retort or storage. That's why the plastic outside of an OnTech container is really a composite of six layers of material, even though it doesn't feel that way in your hand.

You have a smooth plastic material on the very outside of the can; then you have a recycled plastic material attached to that layer; then you have a layer of adhesive that binds the recycled plastic to a very thin layer of ethyl vinyl alcohol (EVOH). Traveling further inward, you have another layer of adhesive, which bonds the EVOH to a final layer of smooth plastic.

The problem is that you have to take this composite and attach it to the top and bottom of the can, which is accomplished with a technique called double-seaming. We're talking about how that little rim on the top of a soda can is formed.

Even though the OnTech team had optimized the design for the can parts, it hadn't optimized the way in which the can shell was attached to the can lid. They needed the can itself to be lower cost, but the can had to have all those layers also. (See Figure 14-2.)

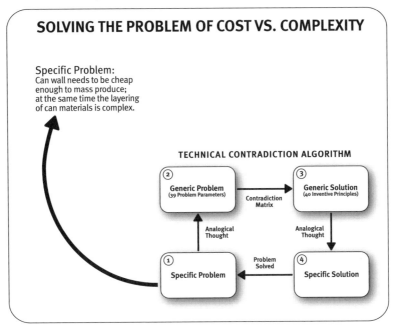

SOLVING THE PROBLEM OF COST VS. COMPLEXITY

Specific Problem:
Can wall needs to be cheap
enough to mass produce;
at the same time the layering
of can materials is complex.

TECHNICAL CONTRADICTION ALGORITHM

② Generic Problem (39 Problem Parameters) → Contradiction Matrix → ③ Generic Solution (40 Inventive Principles)

Analogical Thought

① Specific Problem ← Problem Solved ← ④ Specific Solution

14-2: The challenge for OnTech was to find a solution to more than 400 technical problems, or contradictions. Just one of these problems is highlighted here.

Then someone had a brilliant idea. Oh no, sorry — that's the way innovation usually happens, if it happens at all.

In this case, there was a technical contradiction at play: The useful feature of low-cost manufacturing was in conflict with the harmful feature of high product complexity, relative to its purpose and nature. With this defined, the technical team could now match the nature of its specific problem with Altshuller's 39 generic problem parameters, which it did, like this:

	OnTech's Specific Problem	Generic Problem Parameter
Useful Feature	Has to be cheap enough to mass produce	Ease of manufacturing (#32)
Harmful Feature	Layering of materials is complex	Complexity of device (#36)

The next step was using the contradiction matrix to locate the inventive principles that correspond to the generic parameters of the problem. Cross-referencing ease of manufacturing (#32) with complexity of device (#36) yields the following inventive principles: Inexpensive short-life object (#27), use of copies (#26), and segmentation (#1), as shown in the graphic:

	Harmful Feature	Complexity of Device (#36)
Useful Feature		
Ease of Manufacturing (#32)		27, 26, 1

APPLICABLE INVENTIVE PRINCIPLE

Number one, Segmentation, was the principle that focused the team on an appropriate solution to its technical problem. By further segmenting a step in the manufacturing process, the complexity of the material would stay the same, but the cost would go down. No longer would OnTech use precision blow-molding to attach the sides and ends of the can; it would use a more imprecise method that's much cheaper, and then use die stamps to cut the rough material into perfect shape. The process added a step, cost went down, and complexity remained constant. (See Figure 14-3.)

Another contradiction that had to be solved brings you to the core of the can where the energy reaction happens. Inasmuch as the outside of the can *should not* be conductive, the inside part that houses the reaction *should be* conductive. You want as much energy to pass through the inside wall as possible to heat your drink. But at the same time, you have to protect the drink and the chemistry (calcium oxide) from oxygen ingress.

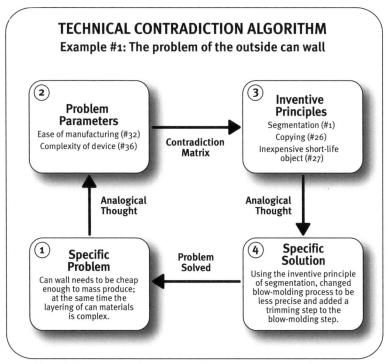

TECHNICAL CONTRADICTION ALGORITHM
Example #1: The problem of the outside can wall

14-3: OnTech moved from a specific problem to a specific solution by working through the four steps of the innovation algorithm in this manner.

Therefore, the team had the same problem it had before about oxygen ingress, but this time it was different. This time, the team had to keep oxygen out of the product with a barrier that was energy conductive, not resistant, as is the outside wall of the can. Here's how it broke down:

	OnTech's Specific Problem	Generic Problem Parameter
Useful Feature	Inside wall has to be strong enough to survive retort	Strength (#14)
Harmful Feature	Inside wall has to be energy conductive while keeping oxygen out too	Temperature (#17)

Verily, this lead to the following inventive principles: flexible shells and thin films (#30), preliminary action (#10), and use of composite materials (#40). The last, use of composite materials, proved to hold the key, as shown in the graphic:

Useful Feature	Harmful Feature Temperature (#17)
Strength (#14)	30, 10, (40)

APPLICABLE INVENTIVE PRINCIPLE

Knowing what they know, the tech team hypothesized that maybe certain combinations of materials could be conductive while also blocking oxygen ingress. One idea, which turned out to be a good one, was to combine ceramic and carbon fiber with plastic, and to take out the EVOH oxygen barrier. It turned out that these elements were in fact strong enough to survive retort, conductive enough to heat the beverage, and oxygen proof too. The composite was implemented and OnTech had its can. (See Figure 14-4.)

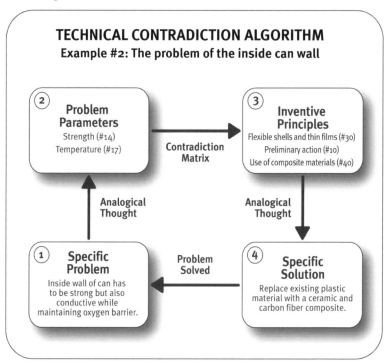

14-4: OnTech moved from a specific problem to a specific solution by working through the four steps of the innovation algorithm in this manner.

As simplistic as we've made the OnTech case seem, its innovation accomplishment was no small task, and TRIZ provided an engine for acceleration on a number of fronts. In fact, years before it was doing its research and development, American National Can (ANC) had completed work on its Omni-Bowl project, which addressed certain of the same issues that OnTech addressed with its product — but not the innovative self-heating aspects.

ANC is a large flexible-packaging company with about 2,000 different products, and tens of millions of investment later, its Omni-Bowl project yielded some important breakthroughs. One such breakthrough was figuring out how to bind metal and plastic into a container seam that would survive retort. None, however, were as technically demanding or as innovative as the ones the OnTech team came up with in their labs at a cost of a small fraction of the ANC solution.

The biggest reason for this was because TRIZ gave the OnTech inventors a small handful of paths to travel, rather than an infinite number of possible paths. We've already discussed what happens when you trade rationally targeted convergence for limitless divergence. Basically you end up in the weeds.

Although it might seem good at first to diverge all over the place, its better to Define the course, Model the variables, Abstract the problem, Solve it with analogical thought, and Implement your solution (TRIZ methodology). With this roadmap, a TRIZ problem-solver or team can make the course of convergence a valuable reality.

Part Two: Resolving Problematic Contradictions

Business as Usual Versus Business as Exceptional

Business as Usual	Business as Exceptional
Improvement project ROI model	Innovation project ROI model
Limited problem-solving opportunity	Unlimited problem-solving opportunity
Define problems as objectives to be achieved (that is, "reduce cost")	Describe specific problems as contradictions to be resolved (for example, "Make cylinder stronger but lighter).
My problems are unique	Someone has solved my problem before, and I can find it and adapt a solution
Analogical process is guided by personal power	Analogical process is guided by robust historical database
Two-step problem solving (trial and error)	Four-step problem solving (specific problem, generic problem, generic solution, specific solution)
Forward from existing	Backward from perfect
Accept compromise and diverge on a solution	Accept ideal and converge on the ideal solution
Ad hoc innovation	Methodological Innovation (DMASI)
Most resources overlooked	All resources exploited
Traditional modeling (flowchart, value stream mapping, etc.)	Innovative modeling via Function Modeling, Substance-Field Modeling, Many-Little-People Modeling

Practical Advice

- Utilize the ideal resolution of a problem or scenario to drive the innovation process.

- Use the concept of contradiction in problem definition and refuse to accept trade-offs or compromise.

- Couple trial-and-error innovation with systematic innovation (as it is repeatable, predictable, and reliable).

- Solve problems using the knowledge of those that proceeded you—TRIZ does this for you.

- Don't accept compromise or trade-offs in planning for and enacting innovation projects.

- Adopt the DMASI methodology as the roadmap for achieving intentional innovation in products and services.

- Tollgate the DMASI methodology to make data-based decisions about continuing or killing innovation projects.

- Tollgate the DMASI methodology to ensure the proper use of TRIZ tools, methods, techniques, and capabilities.

- Don't solve primary problems only to be defeated by secondary problems (win the battle but lose the war).

- Integrate the TRIZ (DMASI) methodology with other existing methods of improvement, innovation, and design (DMAIC, DMADV, etc.).

Endnotes

17 Gary, Loren, "Broadening the Brand," *Innovation Handbook* (Harvard Business School Publishing, 2004), p. 19.

18 Ibid.

19 Ibid.

20 Ibid.

21 CMP Media LLC, *Optimize*, Strategic Innovation section, July 1, 2003, p. 71.

22 Global News Wire, *The Economic Times of India*, Coleman & Co Ltd., March 21, 2003.

23 This idea of searching in far-away places for innovation truth has been developed by many theorists and innovators over time. Perhaps the highest-profile and most popularized voice is that of Henry Chesbrough, whose concept of "open innovation" is perfectly aligned with Altshuller's thinking. Open Innovation (2003) says the chances are great that other people in other industries have solved your problem before.

24 Gavetti, Giovanni and Rivkin, Jan, "How Strategists Really Think: Tapping the Power of Analogy," *Harvard Business Review*, April, 2005, p. 54.

25 In addition to physical and technical, some contradictions are "administrative" in nature, which means they are based on such typical constraints as time, cost, or logistics. Due to the overwhelming presence of available methods to resolve this type of contradiction, it is not addressed with TRIZ tools.

26 Substance-Field Modeling is also used to resolve physical contradictions.

27 This four-stage algorithm can be expressed mathematically as:

Specific problem: $ax^2 + bx + c = 0$;

Generic problem: $3x^2 + 5x + 2 = 0$

Generic solution: $x = \frac{1}{2}\left[-b \pm \sqrt{b^2 - 4ac}\right]$;

Specific solution: $x = -1, -\frac{2}{3}$.

28 A more technical case study of the Ontro self-heating beverage container can be found at www.triz-journal.com.

Part Three:
Crafting an Innovation Roadmap

What the Eight Evolutionary Principles of TRIZ
teach you about planning for strategic breakthrough,
and how they can be applied to predict and create the future.

"It's not enough to create new products. You need to build the prototype of the continuously innovating company."

—John Seely Brown

15
Evolution Won't be Denied

At this point we've covered the basic elements of TRIZ, and we've explored a little about how its empirical nature solves specific technical challenges. But if innovation is to become more pervasive and predictable, it also needs an empirically based managerial framework.

Let's consider the evolution of quality improvement, which started out as a method for improving specific products, and then expanded into services, process, and organizational advancement. While at first improvement methods were myopically focused on the "business of quality," later they evolved into an expansive system that improved the "quality of business."[29]

You can use TRIZ to solve technical contradictions the same way you once used quality to solve operational problems — in a case-by-case, microcosmic way. This is what you might call the "business of innovation." But if business is a function of improvement *and* innovation — and it is — then the act of innovation needs to become a corporate drive as well as a product-level drive. In short, you want to move the innovation cheese from the laboratory to the boardroom. You want to be just as concerned about the innovation of business as you are about the business of innovation.

When scanning the list of major corporate initiatives developed over the past 20 years, you can see a pattern. At first, the corporation has some lofty goals like reducing defects and managing inventory. Then certain tools are developed and tactically enacted to accomplish these goals. The tools that are the most successful become elevated to the status of Strategic Hammer, and they are adopted by many companies across many industries. Finally, these previous sources of competitive advantage become commoditized and incorporated into the general baseline of how organizations do business.

In Part One, we summarize this phenomenon along the lines of the drive for productivity, quality, and innovation. We also say that TRIZ has the lineage and substance to move innovation into a structured state, because it is viable at both the tactical and strategic levels. We spend a little time discussing and demonstrating the gap that exists in business today: Although there is a lot of activity around innovation, it tends to be splintered rather than integrated into a structured framework. The language spoken by innovation strategists is different from the language spoken by innovation technicians. Even amongst the different disciplines of science and engineering, the language and practice of innovation varies greatly.

A big part of converging on an innovation tour de force is to align its tactical and strategic aspects, and this will inevitably happen. Many companies now create innovation roadmaps, institute their associated plans, and implement projects according to these strategies and plans. But we question the quality of those roadmaps and plans, just as we have questioned the quality by which most go about innovating at the product level. And we question the ability of most corporations to coordinate the strategic and tactical aspects of innovation in a way that optimizes resources.

But before the synergy of strategic and tactical innovation can occur, a corporation has to understand the macro forces of evolution — just like the innovation practitioner has to understand the micro forces. A company has to manage the overall progression of innovation in general, not just execute the specific steps of creative problem solving.

Therefore, if you're an innovation champion, by what method do you assess the maturity of your current technology? How do you predict when the net profitability of your products and services will become squeezed to the point of commoditization? By what logic and empirical method do you build an innovation roadmap for your organization? How do you select appropriate and viable innovation projects?

Here again, Altshuller has something to say, because he once asked these same questions. Using some of the same and some new research to derive his technical taxonomies, Altshuller derived eight patterns by which any system evolves, and these eight patterns can be decomposed into more than 400 separate lines, each with their own unique signature.[30] No, technological systems don't evolve randomly but according to

Eight Classic Patterns of Evolution

1. Evolution toward Increased Ideality.
2. Stages of Evolution of Technology.
3. Non-Uniform Development of System Elements.
4. Evolution toward Increased Dynamism and Controllability.
5. Increased Complexity then Simplification (Reduction).
6. Evolution with Matching and Mismatching Elements.
7. Evolution toward Micro-level and Increased Use of Fields.
8. Evolution toward Decreased Human Involvement.

set objective patterns, universal trends that give insight into how products, services, and whole organizations change over time.

The underlying natures of different technical problems in different domains at different times are essentially the same, and this is why TRIZ is tactically necessary. But inasmuch as you can't afford to ignore the generic patterns of technical breakthrough (micro), you certainly can't ignore the generic patterns of organizational evolution (macro), and in this sense, TRIZ is as much strategic as it is tactical in nature. Therefore, the eight evolutionary patterns of TRIZ, shown in the "Eight Classic Patterns of Evolution" sidebar (p. 63), shed equal light on the technical and managerial worlds. In both domains, the knowledge of these patterns is useful in guiding decision making, goal setting, resource planning, and risk management.

You can think of the eight patterns of evolution as different lenses through which to view the trajectory of technology and systems. In a broad sense, that's what technology really is: the arrangement of hardware, software, processes, and people into a way of creating value. In this sense, value streams, computers, procedures, machines, templates, instructions, and standard practices are all forms of technology. A bicycle is technology, and so is a car, or a spaceship. An electrical circuit design is technology, as is a CAD drawing for a building. Same with the configuration of technologies in your home - all of which require design, construction, maintenance, and, most illustratively, renewal.

Here's how it works: Know-how and technique combine with machinery and tools to power an endless stream of evolution toward the next iteration of how companies can meet human needs. One discovery or development combines with another, and the process of planning, building, optimizing, and reinventing unfolds. As technique and know-how unfold into an endless stream of adaptation and innovation, humans evolve in line with their creations. Therefore, we drive innovation as much as it drives us, in never-ending symbiosis. Our bodies, minds, and spirits change as they interact with the creations we've made.

The Strategic TRIZ Methodology

Strategic TRIZ is a structured approach to predicting and planning the evolution of systems. It follows a progression of Define, Map, Apply, Plot, and Implement (DMAPI):

DEFINE the existing conditions and parameters in the system to create the baseline for forecasting. Business and market analysis is appropriate at this phase, as well as a historical synopsis of evolution to date inside and outside the company.

MAP maturity with data collected from major descriptor categories: financial, patents, innovative level of patents, primary performance characteristics, harmful functions (risk), and others as necessary. The mapping technique determines the configuration of investment for 1) expanding the net profitability of current system lifecycles and

(continued)

As thrilling as it is to envision the future, it's disturbing that business leaders can't always make it happen. Or maybe people just don't envision it very well, because they're so buried in the specific matter of their own organizations. In any industry, rare is a view of evolution that steps outside the bounds of specific industry language, knowledge, and practice. With strategic TRIZ, you step beyond the realm of the particular into the realm of the abstract, just as you did with TRIZ at the tactical level. With tactical TRIZ, you use a very finite set of parameters and principles to solve a technical innovation problem. With strategic TRIZ, you use a very finite set of generic patterns to solve the managerial problem of "where do we go next from here?"

It's the same idea all over again. Do you want to keep chasing after the brilliant strategists — the leadership equivalent of the mad scientist — for the wisdom of how to reinvent the corporation? Or do you want to make a force of people who know how to think strategically at the fundamental level? You want to do the latter without sacrificing the former.

Peter Drucker, Gary Hamel, Michael Hammer, and many others have talked about the difference between continuous and discontinuous change, and have coached businesses through the process of "changing the rules of the game." And the likes of Alvin Toffler (*Future Shock, Third Wave*) have described the patterns of global change in terms of trends, synthesized realities, and predictive statements. This is all good, because the major currents of change, in all their many sectors and combined forms, are necessary material for the strategist's brain.

But for all the great strategic thinking, what have people learned about innovation, and how can you reflect that back on yourself to innovate better? This is the scientist's question, and if the scientist bothers to ask a question about business, maybe it's a good idea to listen. After all, science drives business as much as business drives science, because they exist symbiotically. The strategic TRIZ practitioner asks what

---

2) creating new lifecycle curves.

APPLY patterns of evolution to create a technology roadmap that identifies overlooked areas of opportunity, as well as opportunities for hybridization. Apply each of the Patterns of Evolution and predict evolutionary stages based on this application. Build the future state of the roadmap and identify constraints and feasibility data for each potential path, and for combined paths.

PLOT the multi-generational product plan (MGPP) by identifying specific evolutionary paths based on the confluence of relevant data streams. Create a composite plan that identifies several generations of development, stages their implementation, and coordinates them with market readiness.

IMPLEMENT the innovation roadmap in conjunction with strategic planning, improvement, and innovation tools. Compare the impact of the roadmap with predicted values identified in the Define phase to confirm the demanded ROI.

programming code lies under the activity of strategic thinking and innovation. And this brings you right back to the eight evolutionary patterns, because they are the code behind the thinking. They are the gauge that tells you if your thinking is synergized with the *way things are,* as far as you know them.

16
Mapping Your Maturity

Wrapped around the eight evolutionary patterns is a measurable framework for planning, executing, and evaluating strategic innovation, because you need this as much as you need a framework for managing the technicalities of innovation. Therefore, you have the tactical TRIZ methodology of DMASI, but you also have the strategic method of Define-Map-Apply-Plot-Implement (DMAPI), summarized in "The Strategic TRIZ Methodology" sidebar (pp. 64-65). In the big picture of business, the DMAPI methodology is a direct input into the Strategic Thinking process, which synthesizes a host of critical success factors in formulating the ideal state of an organization.

Essentially, the DMAPI methodology is used to systematically move a business or technical planning team through the stages of technology roadmap development. As we've said, doing so injects more predictability into system performance, whether that system is a process, product, or an organization. With greater predictability around net profitability periods, you can be more deliberate about accordingly planning for improvement and innovation.

Perhaps the R&D department takes the lead in executing DMAPI, or perhaps it does so in conjunction with the executive leadership team. Regardless of who owns and drives it, strategic TRIZ is the mechanism through which you can assess the current state of innovation in the organization, create an innovation plan or roadmap, implement that plan, and evaluate its success. To do this, the strategic TRIZ practitioner first has to develop a *maturity map* of any system or collection of systems, which could be an entire organization.

Every system or functional aspect of a system has primary performance characteristics that can be plotted over time, and it usually looks something like Figure 16-1. This is the classic S-curve, in which the life of some force begins at a snails pace for a long time, dramatically turns upward for a short time, and then levels off or even declines in the later stages of maturity.

Global population is a good example, which rose at an incredibly slow rate from sometime about 10,000 years ago to about 0.5 billion in the year 1750. Since then, in less than 300 years, we've gone from 0.5 billion to more than six billion! Of course, the current exponential population growth has to stop somewhere, because the earth can't support 48 billion people, which is what it would have to do in 120 years if the current rate continues unabated. But you know it won't, because the S-curve eventually flattens at the top.

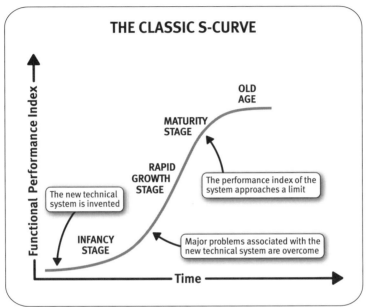

THE CLASSIC S-CURVE

16-1: Every system travels a similar path of slow early momentum, rapid acceleration, and then significant slow down. After this, the system is made generally obsolete by a newly innovated system that does what the old one did much better, faster, and cheaper.

What you don't know is when the top of the S-curve will come for population, the stock market, the growth of a company, the profitability of a product or service. Yet it seriously behooves you to forecast, especially if your job is to run a company, because all systems behave in an S-curve way: They have a stage of infancy that creeps along until barriers are removed and problems are solved.

Then the system performs according to some path of rapid improvement until it approaches a limit, at which time its societal and economic value declines, even to the point of having little or no value at all. As new systems are introduced, they leapfrog past the old way of meeting some human need, and this renders the old way obsolete.

A good example is the system known as "finding the information you need," which used to follow the rules of bricks and mortar. If you wanted information, you had to go to a library somewhere, period. There were no other options, because all public information was stored in libraries, and only in libraries. So we've made libraries as efficient as possible, indexing books and magazines, first in physical Rolodexes® and later on, computers.

Although this search-and-retrieve system was getting better and faster, the technology of the PC converged with the technologies of networks, and the Internet was born. All of a sudden, you could sit at home and search the many sources of information about your topic in a split second. Because of this, the cycle time of getting what you needed went down dramatically, of course with the added pain of maybe getting way more hits than you wanted. Further, quite unlike the library model, the new way does not require you to return the information after you're done using it.

Anyone who was in the business of finding and selling information before had to adapt to the new way. And it didn't take any great mind to figure out that those in the business of selling information, like magazines, would have to make their information available online, not just through snail mail and libraries.

What did take vision, however, was to anticipate this shift before it happened based on a belief in the inevitable. The PC began its radical ascent into every business and household in the 1980s, and so did computer networks. So why could hardly anyone really predict that these two separate technologies were destined to converge into what they are today? Why couldn't all the companies see the inevitable shift and prepare for it, even lead it?

Why couldn't you see all those people shopping, asking Jeeves, or paying their bills online? Today, you can go to Google and get whatever information you want, and lots of it. But what's next for Google? If Google doesn't figure it out, who will? Who will bring the next wave of change for meeting the human need for getting information?

Someone will and, even so, that's not the point, because simply knowing some emerging technology is on the way won't help you plan for it. It doesn't take intelligence to know that change is coming, even big change, because it will. However, it does take a unique individual to predict with some accuracy when and how change will happen.

Without getting too philosophical, change in business is a function of spawning and converging products, services, and transactions. Although they all exist to meet the same basic human needs, they do so in endlessly evolving permutations. So the core competency business needs today is people who can size up the lifecycles of all these ways and predict when they will wear out, need to be improved, or need to be cannibalized with innovation.

This is the strategic value of TRIZ: It enables the mapping of all critical system lifecycles such that the business can make better decisions about which systems to improve, which to innovate, and which to retire. If you know this, you know a lot about how to select and focus various business tools, like Six Sigma or Lean or CRM. In fact, you have a framework within which to pretty much do everything with a little more certainty.

Maturity Mapping generally works by plotting the functional lifecycle of a system, which could be a product, process, service, transaction, or organization. Then you plot the net profitability period of that system, along with such other curves as "number of inventions over time," or "level of invention over time."

For example, if you apply this framework to the organization itself, its functional performance characteristic might be described and measured in terms of its mission. The number of innovations is just that, although the level of innovations refers to the extent to which they deviate from the norm on the continuum from extremely continuous to extremely discontinuous. Finally, system profitability is plotted along with other factors.

It shouldn't take long to see the important relationships between the curves shown in Figure 16-2 for one stylized system. In reality, such

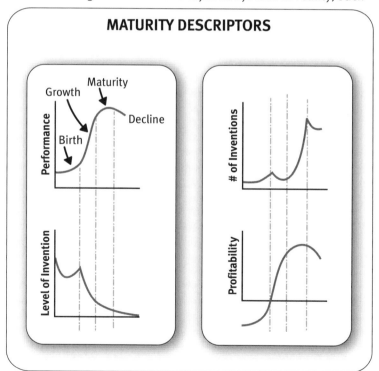

16-2: An organization can use any number of metrics to understand where it is on the S-curve of functional performance relative to any given system, macro or micro in nature. It can also use these metrics, or descriptors, to predict when a given system will reach certain evolutionary milestones and, accordingly, construct its research and development plans.

lifecycle curves for any system show specific correlations between their functionality, profitability, productivity, and quality dimensions at certain points in time. Other factors can be mapped too, such as the harmful functions, or risk, inherent in a system or an organization. Although the guiding frame of the process is Maturity Mapping, the real formulation of the innovation roadmap occurs by using the eight inventive patterns to predict the evolutionary stages of a product or system.

17

The Eight Patterns Described

The first of Altshuller's eight evolutionary patterns is *evolution toward increased ideality*, which asserts that every system generates both useful effects and harmful effects. For example, the system known as a car usefully gets you from point A to point B, but it does so while harming the environment to some extent. Over time, the car has evolved in a way that has increased its useful effects while decreasing its harmful effects. Therefore, the goal for any system is to maximize the ratio of useful to harmful effects, such that you approach Ideality.

Pattern two is the *stages of technology evolution*, which is essentially the S-curve that forms the basis of the Maturity Mapping framework. A product or system is conceived in the mind and lingers there until it reaches a point of reality. Then an invention is made to meet some need, but it has numerous unsolved problems and contradictions.

After this, society recognizes the value of the new system, and investment is made to overcome its problems and contradictions — its barriers to commercialization. This is the time when the S-curve turns sharply upward and profitability grows as lower level inventions and optimization efforts push the new wave of change to its limit. System development slows, small improvements are made, and profitability levels or starts to decrease.

Personal computers are a good example of this non-linear progression from system initiation to system commoditization or extinction. When PCs first became available, they were expensive and problematic, and it was difficult to make money selling them. But then technology and demand converged, and the PC industry moved dramatically from early adoption to mass adoption.

Today, however, PC technology has reached a limit of profitability, marked by the wave of change brought on by the Internet. Yes, many more people still need PCs, and the Internet only drives PC sales, but the profitability associated with strictly making PCs is highly constrained, because the process has been optimized and commoditized.

Without innovation, mature systems are lucky to eek out a living, and maybe this is what Dell saw when it decided to change the way PCs are ordered, built, stocked, shipped, and serviced. The strategic minds at Dell saw the S-curve of the PC and figured it was time to change the rules. So they built a new model within which to make, sell, and service desktop computers — thereby extending profitability around its commoditized products.

We should note that this move by Dell is a lower-level innovation, because the basic technology of the PC has not changed for quite some time. And other S-curves are in full force, such as the one that represents all the handheld computer devices, or the one that's experimenting with embedding computing devices in watches, eyeglasses, clothing, and who knows what else. You can be sure there are a few people at Dell who are looking at these curves with predictive eyes.

The third of Altshuller's inventive patterns is the *non-uniform development of system elements*, which purports that each system component has its own S-curve. Therefore, different components evolve on their different schedules, reaching their inherent limits at different times. In turn, this creates contradictions and/or constraints, as certain components can hold back the progress of the whole system.[31]

The strategic TRIZ practitioner analyzes systems to discover constraining components. The tactical TRIZ practitioner then uses the contradiction resolution process to solve the constraint. Recall that behind every barrier to innovation is really some physical or technical contradiction, or possibly a family of contradictions. If you can solve the contradiction, you can leapfrog beyond its associated limits.

Inventive pattern four is *evolution toward increased dynamism and controllability*, which means that, as systems become more flexible over time, they also become easier to monitor. You see this in manufacturing, where the ability to interchange machinery and parts has been met with the ability to control process capability. Another example is the increased dynamism you see between customers and providers, enabled by Internet-based transaction ware. Looking at your account online, trading stocks, buying books — all these increase relational dynamism while improving the control of that interaction.

If you lead a transactional business, you look underneath your specific product and service portfolio; you look at the tectonic patterns of evolution that are pushing your systems along. Therefore, if the world is always moving toward increased dynamism and controllability, you want to tap into that movement. In a way this is the Tao of business: listening to the voice of Evolution and letting it tell you what to do. This way, you're flowing with the wind, not against it.

Why not compare running a business with the spiritual quest of listening to the inner voice? All spiritual people say that this is the way of happiness and fulfillment. If your mind is quiet enough, the universe will tell you who you are and what you are to do. Analogously, the eight patterns of evolution are the universal voices that tell you what to do in the midst of apparent chaos — but only if the strategic mind is quiet and *inactive* enough to hear them.

The fifth evolutionary pattern is *increased complexity, then simplification*, which is the tendency for systems to add functions that at first increase complexity but over time become collapsed into simpler systems that provide the same or more functionality. For example, cameras became more complex when such functions as focusing and flashes were added. But later, these functions were integrated and automated into systems that provided multi-functional capability.

Once there was a time when pizza parlors decided it was a good idea to deliver, so some functions were added, like taking orders, transcribing addresses, and dispatching drivers. The system added complexity to provide greater functionality. When you call into a pizza place now, it likely has an automated system that recognizes your phone number, displays your address, and identifies the types of pizza you've ordered lately. Increased complexity collapsed into greater simplicity and, again, the key is to predict when and design how it's best to make this happen in an organization.

Pattern number six is *evolution with matching and mismatching elements*, which says that evolving system elements are matched or mismatched to improve performance or compensate for undesired effects. Therefore, it's the configuration of elements that sometimes holds the secret to how you can either extend the lifecycle of a system or cannibalize it with a new one.

Simply, matching elements are those that have the same functional nature. So a vacuum cleaner that utilizes suction might evolve from constant suction to pulsating suction to resonance pulsation and so on. Then, the act of suction in any of these forms might be augmented with a rotor brush — the spinning brush part of the power nozzle. The addition of the rotating brush is a matching-element evolution, because it adds a part that enhances only the one function of suction.

An example of evolution with mismatching elements is the suspension system of a vehicle, or the way the wheels of a vehicle are attached to its body. The function of rolling and the function of passenger comfort exist in the same system, and they need to be connected in a way that enhances both to the greatest extent possible.

Back in that day, the wheels of covered wagons were bolted directly to the body of the vehicle, and the resulting ride was pretty bumpy. And the earliest automobiles, steam and combustion, had only rudimentary systems for evolving this line of mismatching functional elements. Of course, today you have cars with sophisticated suspension systems that self-adjust according to road conditions.

Let's visit the seventh pattern, *evolution toward the micro level and increased use of fields*, which says that technological systems tend to transition from macro systems to micro systems, and that different types of energy fields are used to achieve better performance and control during this transition.

Remember when a computer was a huge system of mechanical card reading? Well probably not, if you're younger than 60. The field used for computing shifted from mechanical to electrical, and the machines got a lot smaller. The same is true of systems that transition from, say, thermal energy to atomic energy. We saw this when we instituted nuclear power as an alternative to thermally combusting coal and oil, and the space needed to perform the function got smaller.

Generally speaking, a system evolves toward increasingly smaller energy fields, beginning with the field of mechanical interaction and progressing all the way to the field of electromagnetic interactions, which are the smallest of all in size. We're talking about the size difference between the hinges on your door (mechanical) and the radiation of an X-ray (electromagnetic). In between, you have the fields of thermal, molecular, chemical, electrical, and magnetic. It's important for the TRIZ expert to know how these fields connect in the same system and how systems tend to evolve toward the most microcosmic level possible.

Finally, the eighth and final evolutionary pattern is *evolution toward decreased human involvement*, and this one should be immediately obvious to anyone. Washing machines, remote controls, power windows, cars, and almost everything else in society follows this trend — and some on the wild fringe are convinced it will continue until people can move things around with their minds.

Because all eight evolutionary patterns are networked in nature, one can serve as a funnel for another, and vice versa, depending on the situation. For example, the patterns of *matching and mismatching elements* could help the innovator determine a general pathway of focus. The system might evolve in a way that connects functionally different but codependent elements (mismatches), rather than in a way that taps into the progression of matching elements.

From here, the pattern of *increased complexity, then simplification* could apply as the engineer designs a new system for evolving mismatching elements. At first, the innovative adaptation makes the mismatching system more complex, but later it becomes simpler. And maybe it also becomes smaller as the forces of *evolution toward the micro level and increased use of fields* pattern would dictate.

Although one evolutionary pattern might illuminate the path of innovation better than the others under certain circumstances, it's more likely that most technology development roadmaps will embody more than one of the eight evolutionary patterns. The strategic TRIZ thinker doesn't see technology development as a specific problem to be solved, but as a specific expression of underlying patterns.

It's not about the way the parts are designed, molded, and snapped together that preoccupies the TRIZ strategist. Nor is the TRIZ strategist overly concerned with even the specific customer requirements a system is supposed to meet. Despite MIT professor Eric Von Hippel's and others' call for consumers to be innovation co-creators, they usually don't know what they want or need. Henry Ford said that if he had asked his customers what they wanted, they would have said, "a faster horse."

The pure TRIZ strategist looks at patterns and principles, almost like seeing in another dimension, to configure innovations that meet some underlying societal need. You don't want to know how to increase the bandwidth of the PlayStation so it can meet the customer need of "more realistic gaming." You want to know which patterns of evolution will characterize the next innovative incarnation of what it means to engage in gaming for human entertainment.

This is a subtle distinction, and one we further define in Part Four, when we talk about the limitation of Axiomatic Design in the context of a total performance excellence system. In a nutshell, the task of the innovator is to supplement the classic paradigm of design with a deeper pool of intellectual capital. If the design engineer thinks in terms of customer-based requirements, parameters, and variables, the TRIZ engineer thinks in terms of need-based constructs and innovations.

To bring the conversation around, we use the eight evolutionary patterns to construct a technology roadmap that profiles the life curves of key products and systems. We need the wisdom of maturity mapping, and these patterns, to accurately predict when a product or system will become profitable, and when we can expect profitability to erode. Moreover, we use the patterns of evolution to define the fuzzy edge of what we will be tomorrow compared with what we are today.

18
The Evolution of Six Sigma

Just as we provided an in-depth example of tactical TRIZ in Part Two, we provide a more in-depth view of strategic TRIZ here. However, we readily admit that the maturity of strategic TRIZ as a systematic management practice is not as developed as the maturity of tactical TRIZ. Although the eight evolutionary patterns are perfectly sound, and although the DMAPI methodology is practiced by some, the body of case material around strategic TRIZ is indeed thin. But that was once the case for any number of methodologies before they found traction on the S-curve of their development.

Because this is a book about a management methodology, we thought it might be useful to illustrate some aspects of strategic TRIZ and the eight evolutionary patterns by tracing the etiology of business excellence from the early days of organizational life. All the management discoveries of the past 100 years have been catalogued into some integrated framework or consciousness of business excellence. One piece builds on the next in the never-ending cycle to create and deliver more value per unit of investment. Scientific discovery evolves, technology progresses, business systems get more sophisticated, and methodologies of performance excellence become more commoditized.

The cycle runs unabated, as it should, and choices expand, just as they do at the level of the individual product, which is where management can learn a valuable lesson from the technical community. In the product domain, you see a great divergence of options within the confines of converging standards and technology. Thousands of ideas are developed, but only a tiny handful ever make it into production and commercialization. And those that eventually do, according to some algorithm of predictability, converge into no more than a few sets of globally acknowledged standards.

Modern examples of this phenomenon are found in virtually every industry, as business makes profit, as money is invested in R&D, as technology converges, and as options diverge within converged global standards. From time to time, certain waves of innovation combine to create a synthesized manifestation of technologies, and the new hybrid becomes the new standard. One example of this is the video phone. Once a cell phone without video capability was the accepted baseline, but now, if your phone doesn't have a camera, it's inferior.

Once it was the baseline to implement some kind of TQM-style quality program, just like once it was considered leading-edge to implement Just in Time or Quality Function Deployment, or to design a management system with hierarchically cascaded objectives, a system of metrics and regular review cycles. As these methodologies evolved, practitioners added new capabilities and functions, and the basal set of intellectual property and know-how grew, even multiplied.

For example, the roots of what would 80 years later be called TQM were planted in 1908, when W.S. Gosset developed statistical tests to help analyze quality data obtained at Guinness Brewery. About the same time, A.K. Erlang studied telephone traffic problems for the Copenhagen Telephone Company in an effort to increase the reliability of service in an industry known for its inherent randomness. It's likely that Erlang was the first mathematician to apply probability theory in an industrial setting, an effort that lead to modern queuing theory and reliability theory.[32]

And it's important to mention Walter Shewhart, who in the 1930s worked with Bell Labs to develop the theoretical concepts of quality control, who developed the Shewart Cycle (Plan-Do-Check-Act), and who was the mentor of W. Edwards Deming, the undisputed father of modern quality control. Also working with Bell Labs was Dodge and Romig, who pioneered the practice of acceptance sampling.[33]

Then it was the Japanese in the 1940s and 50s, with the help of Edwards Deming and Joseph Juran, who began to pioneer these elements of quality control into a teachable, learnable, and doable system called Statistical Quality Control (SQC). The DNA of quality control had congealed into a systematic structure that could be institutionalized.

In the domain of managing performance excellence, just as in the domain of managing individual products and services, added features and functionality create more complexity for the producer and the consumer. Over time, however, complexity gives way to more simplicity as engineers find ways to integrate systems and designs for more simplistic manufacturing and use by consumers. That's why the computer and printer you could buy ten years ago was incredibly more expensive and inferior to the one you can buy today.

Within the TRIZ world, another way of looking at the fifth pattern of evolution *(increasing complexity, then simplicity)* is in terms of hybridization. As a system gets more functionality and gets more complex, it splinters into more and different parts. But over time, the added functionality collapses or hybridizes back into a simpler design.

You see this happen in manufacturing repeatedly as systems add part counts during the period of increasing functionality, then reduce part counts as designs are simplified to provide the same functionality.

Take a pencil for example. In the beginning it was just a piece of wood with a length of black lead. In the language of a TRIZ practitioner who understands the dynamic progression of hybridization, this simple writing system is a "homogeneous mono-system." Then when someone added an eraser to the pencil, it was transformed from a homogeneous mono-system to a "heterogeneous bi-system." That is, the pencil performed two different functions, writing and erasing, within the same system.

After more time, mechanical pencils could incorporate different colors of lead so you could write in black, red, green, and blue — using the same instrument. In TRIZ language, you can say that the pencil with the eraser became a heterogeneous poly-system. It performs more than one function by adding more parts and complexity.

But now you have a multi-colored lead pencil that collapses the colors back into one length of lead that, depending on the angle it is held, will write different colors. With this advancement, you now have a new heterogeneous mono-system that writes all the different colors with nearly the simplicity of writing with one color, while providing the eraser, of course.

So with the pencil, you see a very simple illustration of how systems evolve toward increasing complexity and added functionality, and then toward increasing simplicity with no erosion of function.[34] The evolutionary principle of hybridization is universal — meaning it has been validated over and over again. Naturally, in the drive to be better, you try to take the best of one system or technology and mix it with the best of another to get the best of both. This is the perennial drive of the fittest, and it won't be denied.

Another example of hybridization is the work of biologists who engineer the best properties of one system into the best properties of another, while simultaneously canceling the drawbacks of each as they relate to the objective at hand. An old but good example is the cross-breeding of two different plant seeds, one that survives in dry climates, the other that survives in cold places. Although neither could live in a cold, dry place, the hybrid can.

So because of intentional hybridization, the plant is more robust to temperature and moisture, and you can use this principle to explain what happened next in the progression of quality and TQM. After the practice of SQC became solidified as a viable means for improving and controlling manufacturing processes, why couldn't it be applied to other processes as well — in procurement, administrative departments, distribution, and marketing?

What can't the seed grow in more than one climate? Why can't the pencil write in blue and green and not just black? Why can't the principles and practices of quality control be applied outside of manufacturing?

By the force of evolution, SQC expanded and diversified into all departments and functions of an organization, and the Japanese drove it there until Armand Feigenbaum coined the term Total Quality Control, or TQC. The homogenous mono-system (SQC) became a homogeneous poly-system (TQC) as it expanded the function of quality improvement and control to everything an organization does.

Not incidentally, around this same time when the industrial economy was growing rapidly across the globe, others were working to develop so many other aspects of what you now take for granted as the underpinnings of business success.

In Japan in the 1950s, the forefathers of Lean Manufacturing were pioneering the methods of flow, waste reduction, inventory control, and operational speed. In Russia, a team of engineers were developing the empirical basis for product, process, and organizational innovation. Also in Japan, others were developing Hoshin Kanri methods, which quantitatively connect the functions and processes of an organization around strategic priorities.

Fast forward to the 1970s, 80s, and 90s, when certain families of management tools collapsed into themselves, forming simpler and more integrated versions of formerly fragmented systems. By tracing the development of TQM, you arrive at a point in the United States when all the tools of SQC became packaged together for ease of deployment and application into a set of standards known as the Baldrige criteria, and this was really the defining time when the system known as TQM became a big tool itself, a homogeneous poly-system that reduced defects and variation and improved the quality of products and services focused on customer needs.

Still later, the components of TQM were dovetailed with other key systems and practices, such as David Norton and Robert Kaplan's Balanced Scorecard. After all, what good is quality improvement if you can't trace its impact? It was around this time that Motorola began driving hard with a methodology called Six Sigma, which had its beginnings as a big hammer for pounding the nails of product quality to the point of no more than 3.4 defects per million opportunities for defects at the quality characteristic level.[35]

After some evolutionary momentum, Six Sigma extended its data-driven reach to focus on creating significant financial return, first in the form of cost reductions born of process improvements, and later in the form of growth by its application in sales and marketing. In addition,

Six Sigma injected the agenda of quality into the top executive level of corporations, materializing TQM's former lip service to top management involvement.

With a connected system of performance metrics, hard accountability at the executive level, top- and bottom-line impact, and large-scale deployment, Six Sigma achieved the dream of TQM and became the world-class mono system for performance capability.

But for all this, Six Sigma is still just an extension of the quality movement, with new functionality first made more complex but now made simpler and more commoditized through programmed deployment designs, e-learning, and other software aides and technologies. The evolutionary trend of "complex to simple" was augmented with the evolutionary trend of "decreased human involvement," another TRIZ tenet, and you arrive today at a place where Six Sigma can be implemented in an organization with less effort and greater return on investment than ever before.

Part Three: Crafting an Innovation Roadmap

Business as Usual Versus Business as Exceptional

Business as Usual	Business as Exceptional
Reactive evolution	Proactive evolution
The quality of business	The innovation of business
Ad hoc technology roadmap formulation	Classic patterns as guides
Driven by unbridled thinking and strategic genius	Driven by methodology (DMAPI)
Estimate Product/Process maturity	Empirically map maturity
Organizations evolve in response to market pressures	Organizational evolution is predictable and controllable

Practical Advice

- Think and plan strategically so that your innovation efforts support the vision, goals, and objectives of the organization.
- Create the habit of innovation (like Deming and Juran made quality habitual).
- Recognize that all business strategies should push the organization toward one of a finite set of evolutionary principles.
- Plan multiple generations using the patterns of evolution and advanced patent analysis instead of market and competitive pressure.
- Know the net profitability periods of your products and/or services, and control your innovation cycle.
- Appoint and train TRIZ champions who can plan for innovation and quantifiably oversee its implementation.

Endnotes

29 Quoted portions from an interview with Six Sigma inventor and thought leader Mikel Harry.

30 Some TRIZ theorists and practitioners purport 14 inventive principles, but we like eight because they embody the full extent of the 14 without any over complication.

31 This same idea is embodied and expanded by the Theory of Constraints, developed by Eli Goldratt after Altshuller defined this third pattern. The Theory of Constraints basically says that any system, despite its large number of problems and limiting forces, has a single constraint preventing the system from evolution. Uncovering and solving for this constraint successively uncovers the next constraint to solve.

32 Paraphrased from Cox, D.R., "Quality and Reliability: Some Recent Developments and a Historical Perspective,"*Journal of the Operational Research Society*, v41n2, February 1990, p. 95.

33 Ibid.

34 This discussion of hybridization is an extension of TRIZ evolutionary pattern number five, Increased Complexity then Simplification (Reduction).

35 A common misunderstanding of Six Sigma is that it means no more than 3.4 defects per million opportunities for defects at the product level, not at the characteristic level. When you consider this, it becomes easy to understand why Six Sigma quality is so strict yet necessary to achieve. When the probability of defect at the characteristic level cross multiplies across thousands of characteristics in a complex value chain, like the one involved in making a car, the probability of defect at the end of the chain is significantly if not dramatically higher than it is at any one point in the chain.

Part Four:
Enveloping Total Performance

Where structured innovation fits in the framework
of business excellence, and how that framework is enabled
by structured innovation

*"Established companies can develop radical innovations,
and still protect their traditional businesses . . ."*
— Charles A. O'Reilly III and Michael L. Tushman

19
A Simple Construct of Business

In Part One, we take some time to discuss the parallel drives of productivity, quality, and innovation as embodied by various companies and methodologies over time. Then, in Parts Two and Three, we explore in detail how TRIZ enables the drive for innovation at the tactical and strategic levels. In Part Three, we also provide an analysis of how the methods of quality improvement have progressed, combined, and evolved into their most mature form in Six Sigma. Now in Part Four, we present a simple view of business excellence that provides decision-making context for TRIZ, as well as other performance-excellence methodologies.

Back in 1954, Peter Drucker wrote a book called *The Practice of Management,* in which he called out the tendency of corporations to engage in many different programs and initiatives with no integrating system. He called this tendency "the activity trap," and it was his influence that led to the popularity of Management By Objectives (MBO). In a rapidly developing organizational world of proliferating methods and practices, MBO was an integrating force. Its popularity was a naturally occurring phenomenon, because the complexity of management had to converge on a simple framework.

Most companies today practice some form of MBO in an attempt to control operations and bring some level of predictability to their performance. More often than not, however, the MBO framework is just a way of putting audacious goals on the table and holding business leaders accountable for them, regardless of any reasonable approach to setting those goals and selecting the means by which they are achieved.

How does an organization know, in other words, which business methods to deploy and implement from among the large number of choices? When is basic Process Management appropriate to deploy versus a more aggressive improvement thrust like Six Sigma, or Design for Six Sigma (DFSS)? And when is it best to innovate a paradigm shift change with TRIZ, rather than incrementally improve current products, services, and processes?

One truth you know is that an organization shouldn't spin its strategic direction and tactical arsenal based on fanciful dreams or audacious goals. It doesn't take any leadership acumen whatsoever to simply dream the American dream, and then work people to the point of breakdown in trying to make it happen. It does take leadership, however, to circumspectly and scientifically assess current organizational systems in a way that yields valid goals and plans — in a way that enables you to deploy and implement the right tactics and programs at the right times. It's not so much ambition that guides business excellence as it is rightful action at the right times.

American dream aside, a corporation has an identity, just like a person does. And the systems that make a corporation what it is evolve over time, just as people evolve over time. If an organization understands itself — what it is and what it isn't — then it's in a much better position to realize its potential and fulfill its destiny. Not in a big-hairy-goal sort of way, but in a way that's consistent with its natural life path. Therefore, this part of our book lays out a framework within which you can think about the total picture of business excellence before committing to any particular methods or initiatives.

Simply, all of business is the drive to accomplish the mission of the organization better, faster, and cheaper. To make products better, faster, and cheaper. To deliver services better, faster, cheaper. And to operate processes better, faster, and cheaper. (See Figure 19-1.) From a colloquial perspective, that's what all the various management tools do: They play some role in improving quality (better), redesigning processes (better still), spawning reinvention and growth (a lot better), minimizing waste and inventory (faster), reconfiguring operations (faster again), and, of course, cutting costs (cheaper) as a byproduct of all this and a direct result of such targeted initiatives as corporate reorganizations, mergers, and technology implementations.

19-1: Generally speaking, Six Sigma methods make processes and products bettter, while Lean methods make operations faster. Both impact cost and the objectives of each other.

We could depict the general constellation of management tools as intersecting vaccinators of corporate illness. Really, the connected goals of better, faster, and cheaper are all manifestations of some pathology preventing optimum operation, like any pathology that exists in the human body. Everyone has some areas of compromised functioning in their bodies — some part of the spine, some aspect of their organs, some system that is not functioning optimally.

Organizations are no different, as by nature they do not function in an optimal manner. As with anything, like a manuscript or a toy, first you make it, and then you make it better, faster, and cheaper. When you're looking to do this for an entire organization, you need certain values, practices, principles, know-how, and tools.

You need tools of strategic thinking, tools of strategic planning, software tools, data and information tools, improvement tools, basic tools, advanced tools, specialized tools, tools that help you think on the fuzzy edge of innovation, tools that help you conquer new territory, and tools that enable you to occupy the territory you've conquered.

And that's pretty much what you have in the business toolbox today: a veritable explosion of options, just like you have in the world of consumer products and services. And although this represents potential power, it also causes confusion and competition, as champions of Lean, Six Sigma, ISO, Customer Relationship Management, Reengineering, Continuous Improvement, or any number of other initiatives compete for resources.

Often, the winners are those who best line up their programs with the political climate. If the economy is in a downturn, a downsizing program might get the dollars that day. If a commoditized industry player needs to reinvent itself, innovation with TRIZ might win the money. If the strategic focus is on productivity improvement, some technology implementation will prevail. If processes are in disarray or are sub-optimized, a Process Management tool or tool like Six Sigma will get the billing. If process innovation is the priority, Design for Six Sigma or Reengineering becomes the means.

Here's what Dan Valentino said in 1993 in *Transformation*, a Gemini Consulting publication:

> . . . most firms are buzzing with initiatives. Finance will be doing a value analysis; human resources will be re-working incentives; production will be into TQM; marketing will have a customer focus program, and the MIS guys will be doing a major revamp of the software infrastructure. And all these top-level programs will be echoed by a proliferation of more focused initiatives, each of which will be demanding the same resources, claiming the same results and insisting on priority.[36]

This seems as true today as it was a decade ago: Brute force, not harmony and balance, dictates which programs get funded and which ones don't. So it's no wonder we're seeing the emergence of special management elixirs like Six Sigma and Sarbanes-Oxley. As long as Sarbanes is legislated, and every corporation has a compliance budget, it only makes sense to attach your program to the dollar source.

Nevertheless, moving beyond the visceral judgment that such piggy-

backing is bad, tool hybridizations do represent advancement of management know-how, not regression, because the best of one tool is mixed
with the best of another, even if the blending is opportunistic.

And this is why in the performance-excellence space, you see the
hybrids of Six Sigma and Reengineering, Six Sigma and TQM, Six Sigma
and Sarbanes, and, perhaps most notably, the conjoining of Six Sigma
with Lean. In this latter case of Lean Sigma, the power comes from the
coordination of moving the mean with Lean (faster) and controlling variance with Six Sigma (better) — simply speaking. With Six Sigma and Lean
working in planned synergy, the objectives of business are met with more
certainty, because the force of change is more deliberate and integrated.

20

The Grand Unification of Business

In that same article in 1993, Valentino reports the results of study and
work with major corporations, and says, "We often find that there are as
many as 300 initiatives, that up to 40 percent of managers' time is taken
up with 'programs' of one kind or another; that many have no identifiable
benefits; that those that do, lack a system for measuring whether they
are delivering the benefits, and that very few programs have a time limit.
All of which shows there is an appetite for change, a lot of uncoordinated
energy, but no discernable movement in any direction."

This is what we call *Corporate Brownian Motion:* a lot of uncoordinated
energy but no discernable movement in any direction. The physicist will
know what this means, because the notion of Brownian motion refers
to the phenomenon observed through a microscope when looking at
particles suspended in liquid or gas, as they erratically dart around from
constantly colliding with molecules. There is no predictable direction or
pattern, only activity.

But a lot has evolved since 1993, and it seems there has been a
convergence of methodology and accountability, driven in large part by
ROI-based initiatives like Six Sigma. And in the bigger picture, we can't
underestimate the role of the Internet and enterprise technology in bringing various performance-improvement tools together with software and
rapidly deployable knowledge sets (highly scaleable synchronous and
asynchronous e-learning, coaching, and mentoring systems).

It now seems more possible than ever to twist the many strands of
business success into one great fiber of organizational optimization.
Business success is surely not a function of picking that one Holy Tool,
and of turning it loose. Nor is it a function of spreading resources evenly

across the entire gamut of tools, such that Corporate Brownian Motion is installed and reinforced as an ongoing state. When this happens, you end up fighting the inertia caused by the combinatorial effect of programs that are supposed to break inertia.

For many decades, physicists have not surprisingly been trying to assemble a Grand Unification Theory, which would explain the entire workings of the galaxies and everything in them. Although this is an ambitious, if not unachievable, mission, it's not the probability of success that matters. What matters is that the physicist knows all things are connected in some unimaginably big cause-and-effect web. We believe such a web exists for business and, again, it's not the actual formula that matters. What matters is that we understand the whole has a life of its own beyond the sum of its parts and, therefore, we have to optimize the whole by integrating the parts.

This is a sound pursuit, and surely business leaders should be as passionate about understanding the ins and outs of performance excellence as scientists are about understanding the laws of the universe. If you look at the great influencers of business over the past 50 years and longer, you see a list of such names as Shewhart, Ford, Deming, Drucker, Ono, Gates, Hamel, Womack, Harry, Welch, Walton, and many others. Each one of these holds a key to some important aspect of business improvement — some aspect of how an organization creates and delivers value on an increasingly better, faster, and cheaper basis. And some hold the keys to how a business innovates itself periodically to bring on new and different value propositions, which are then relentlessly improved until the cycle needs to repeat itself again.

The important point is that performance excellence is a holistic phenomenon that can only be sufficiently conceptualized and controlled with holistic thinking and holistic action. You know this to be true, intuitively if not empirically, and you know the very best companies have an integrated framework within which they entwine the activities of Strategy, Improvement, and Innovation on an ongoing basis. (See Figure 20-1.) In other words, if the goal of an organization is to do what it does better, faster, and cheaper, you achieve that goal by optimizing the interplay of Strategy, Improvement, and Innovation.

In a *Harvard Business Review* article, Charles O'Reilly and Michael Tushman coined the term *ambidextrous organization*, which refers to a company that can simultaneously preserve itself through continuous improvement while also evolving itself through innovation.[37] We truly do live in a world where constant improvement — getting better, faster, and cheaper all the time — is a necessary requisite for maintaining competi-

TOTAL PERFORMANCE EXCELLENCE MODEL

Strategic Leadership

STRATEGY

INNOVATION   IMPROVEMENT

Operational Leadership

20-1: All business success is the product of world-class strategy, improvement, and innovation driven by synergistically coordinated strategic and operational leadership.

tive position, because every good organization is always improving what it does. In this same world, an organization also has to periodically and rationally reinvent itself — innovating the next generation of products and processes — if it stands any chance of gaining competitive position.

The ambidextrous organization is one that manages the lifecycle of maximizing return from current products and processes (improvement), while investing that return into developing new products and processes that, as strategy thought leader Gary Hamel puts it, "change the rules of the game" (innovation). With change leadership as the driver, all successful organizations implement some configuration of improvement and innovation — if they are to survive.

Exactly how an organization does this doesn't really matter, as long as it keeps the three major parts of performance excellence in good relations, and as long as it keeps each of the key elements within them in good relations too. This is where we look at combining the many elements of performance excellence into a holistic model where all parts are connected as tightly and consistently as possible. It's not the Grand Unification Theory of Business, with all the mathematical connections made, but it is a start on the path of lean decision making.

What is it really you want to do? You want to remove all the waste and non-value-added actions that result from poor decision-making and mediocre coordination. If you could make better decisions and plans as leaders, and if you knew how to follow through on those plans, those responsible for implementation would be much more successful — and the corporation would be better for it.

Shown in Figure 20-2, We propose an integrated performance excellence model that progresses in a lockstep, as the outputs of one piece

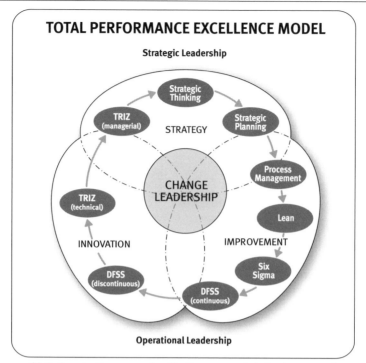

20-2: By adopting a grand unification approach to business excellence, an organization can plan and execute its methodologies in synergistic fashion, instead of suffering the resource drain of "Corporate Brownian Motion." The necessary elements of performance excellence build progressively, where the outputs of one methodology become the inputs for the next. All the elements are balanced, coordinated, and integrated with effective change leadership based on strategic priorities.

become the inputs for the next, driven by change-oriented strategic and operational leadership. The model itself is really no more than a conceptual toolbox within which to organize the various management methods and initiatives. A tool's a tool's a tool, which is why the real value of any tool is in combining it with other tools to construct something of value. Like the human body, and like a product, no one part can work to its potential if the other parts aren't working to theirs.

When you look at the Total Performance Excellence (TPE) model, it should be clear that an organization can populate the main buckets of its toolbox with any number of approaches and methodologies, as per the proliferation of choices, most commoditized, that we've already discussed. We prefer the ones we've shown in the model, because we consider those to have achieved world-class status after so many decades of validation. We also believe that the domains of Strategy and Innovation have a lot to learn from the domain of Improvement, particularly when it comes to making strategy and innovation more methodological, deployable, measurable, predictable, and controllable.

The big deal is in tying all the proven elements of performance success into a coherent system in which all resources and tools are brought to bear on the continuous lifecycle of business evolution. With all the elements of the TPE working in coordinated rhythm, an organization can advance its current and future products, processes, transactions, and services in a way that increases the probability of greater long-term profitability and financial growth.

Therefore, if performance excellence is a function of incremental improvement and breakthrough innovation guided by world-class strategic leadership, what conceptual framework enables us to make this claim? If the TPE model gives us the general progression of approaches and methodologies, what is the general progression of thought that underlies it? As we've been saying all along, in many ways the discipline with which we create and deliver products and services has something to say about the discipline with which we manage our organizations, and so, to answer this question, we turn to MIT professor Dr. Nam Suh, who developed the field of Axiomatic Design.

21

Underpinnings of Total Performance

Dr. Suh's work presents a very logical progression of how you get from a customer requirement to a critical process variable, the performance of which has to be optimized and reliable over time if there is any chance of performance excellence. (See Figure 21-1.) Suh's progression says

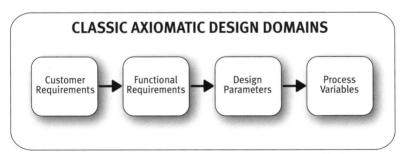

21-1: Effective business activity progresses through several critical stages designed to expedite the time involved and reliability with which an idea moves from "mind to market," or from "concept to cash."

that first you have to identify your customers' needs and requirements using a tool like Quality Function Deployment (QFD) or some combination of effective means. But now you have to convert these customer requirements into functional requirements, because teams of people don't develop customer needs; they develop the functions that meet the customer needs.

But that's not enough either, because you then have to take functional requirements and convert them into the language of the designer and engineer, who talks with words of size, weight, color, and specification — all the many physical aspects of a product or process that, when built or delivered, will provide the functionality that is necessary to meet the customer requirement. Finally, after this, the Axiomatic Design chain ends with the creation of process variables, which drive the manufacturing, transactional, and service competencies that must consistently breath life into the value chain at its most microscopic level.

In a minute, we show you why Dr. Suh's Axiomatic Design framework is the right one on which to hang the pieces of performance excellence. But we also show you why his model is missing a critical piece if it is to power performance excellence in any compelling way on a widespread yet balanced organizational basis. For now, we discuss how the world-class improvement and innovation tools come into play within the closed system of designing how you translate customer requirements into flaw-less operations for meeting those requirements.

On the customer requirement end, we mention using the tool of QFD, which is part of the larger tool, DFSS, which covers the gamut of all four Axiomatic Design domains. You also have Value Stream Engineering, which is instrumental in defining functional requirements, as are the methods of Function Modeling from TRIZ or any number of other ad hoc functional identification techniques. Moving into the design parameter space, DFSS and other tools such as dimensional analysis, tolerance analysis, robust design techniques, and Taguchi's signal-to-noise ratio come into play.

So each of these domains enables the next in progressive fashion, and this gives you a glimpse into a more sequential approach to the networked reality of performance excellence variables. Therefore, a tool like DFSS enables the process variable domain, because if a product or service is designed with high manufacturability or deliverability in mind, the probability of actually making or delivering it reliably increases dramatically.

This is the slingshot effect of avoided error that gets naturally propagated as it rolls through the system. When quality customer requirements are translated into high-quality functional requirements, and when these are translated into high-quality design requirements and, in turn, high-quality quality process variables, there is much less work for methods like DMAIC.

A minute ago, we said we'd point out a limitation with all this, and now we do. We see that Dr. Suh's Axiomatic Design model doesn't really address the strategic components of performance excellence, because it's deliberately focused on operations. So we still need to complete our underlying thought pattern with a domain in front of the customer requirement domain, and let's call that domain "societal need." (See Figure 21-2.)

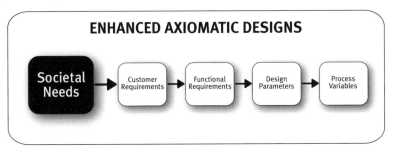

ENHANCED AXIOMATIC DESIGNS

Societal Needs → Customer Requirements → Functional Requirements → Design Parameters → Process Variables

21-2: By adding a domain to the classic Axiomatic Design, we see beyond the limited language of customer requirements, mired as it is in current technology. In other words, we need to think about innovation in terms of underlying societal needs. This is how we move beyond the limitations of current technology and engage in a different conversation about what to develop and commercialize next.

In the history of management hybridization, we're now at the point where we see an interesting rift. Although the tools of improvement have blended well with each other, and have become highly systematized and deployable, the tools of strategy and innovation have not, at least not to the same extent that world-class improvement tools have blended with themselves. Further, all three big domains of Strategy, Improvement, and Innovation have not connected themselves very well, yet some have done well by themselves as evidenced by their market acceptance.

We propose that by adding a domain to the Axiomatic Design model, we can make that model operable as a Grand Unification Theory of Business, again colloquially speaking. The reason is that societal need is the absolute root of business, as all corporations exist to meet the one penultimate objective of fulfilling human needs. Therefore, a company doesn't make watches; it enables people to know the time. This is a very different question for the watchmaker. Maybe there is a way to communicate time that has nothing to do with wearing a contraption on your wrist. TRIZ says there may very well be, if you can get around the contradictions that keep the wristwatch the predominant way to tell time.

In the meantime, customers can't tell you what they need beyond saying they want to know the time. So the conversation and subject of collecting their voice quickly converges on all the many existing time-telling devices and how they might look, feel, and function — ideally. Yet the ideal form, fit, and function — from the customer's perspective — is only an optimization of existing systems, not a revolution of new systems. To revolutionize your business, or your products, you have to back up and live in the box of societal need, and you have to ask more fundamental questions than QFD will lead you to ask.

In Section 6, we highlight the thought process of a medical device maker. In looking for the next innovation, the company's R&D team was preoccupied with making a device that could do its job at a small fraction of its current cost with far less electrical charge. Although this driving framework for innovation was ambitious, it was still contained within the box of current practice. In other words, the possible solutions generated from this team were focused on how to meet customer requirements the way they were defined by the existing system. It wasn't until the team questioned the basic human need met by its device that it opened its paradigm.

Obviously we can't give you any more details to protect our client, but we can say that the team used TRIZ to move away from the domain of customer requirements, which are naturally attached to current technology. When this process was facilitated, the innovation team came up with many possible solutions for meeting the human need that underlies its technology. By doing so, the device maker moved one step closer to realizing the goal of discontinuous breakthrough.

Another company well worth mentioning is Blyth, which holds the Sterno brand in its portfolio. We mention Sterno in Section 5, and describe it as an example of how a company

> ## Sterno® Reinvents Itself
>
> Imagine a non-flammable, safer, more economical alternative to a Sterno gel-filled can – the flaming heat source used at parties to keep food hot.
>
> Using TRIZ, the Sterno Group developed a new, flameless system for heating food. You place two pouches of chemical into a water basin, using the same holding device that's used for Sterno's gel-filled product. The pouches absorb the water to make heat, which warms the food but is not flammable.
>
> The Sterno Flameless™ product is lighter and, therefore, easier to transport, store, and handle than its gel-based, canned alternative.

moves beyond itself into new realms. It's a great story, because Sterno developed a flameless heating pouch that is safer than its more common open-flame product. It also represents technological breakthroughs that were driven by re-asking the fundamental question of how to meet the societal need of keeping food hot. Whereas the entire industry of food-heating devices, and the associated customer requirements, were based on the open-flame model, Sterno shifted the conversation to one of how to keep food hot with no constraints on their thinking.

The interesting aspect of this innovation is that Sterno already held an overwhelming market share advantage when it set about developing the flameless pouch alternative. The best time to evolve and innovate is when you're enjoying great success with your existing products and services. Meeting current customer requirements better than anyone else is the best time to eclipse what you do with an innovation that changes customer requirements in a revolutionary way. Going back to Dr. Nam Suh's work, it's a subtle but critically advantageous shift to make from thinking in terms of customer requirements to thinking in terms of societal need.

This is perhaps the essence of great strategic thinking: knowing that you have boundless opportunity to meet universal human needs in new ways. This fuzzy front edge is where strategic leadership begins, and where the initial concepts are created that then are amplified and materialized by successive performance excellence programs, tools, and methods. Therefore, if the initial concept is weak, that basal strategic intent will compromise the ability of an of an organization to perform throughout the entire value chain.

This is why it's so important to approach performance excellence holistically, and to have methods for defining the fuzzy front edge, just like you have methods for improving process capability and innovating new products and processes. This is where TRIZ methods come in, because the overwhelming majority of methodologies used for idea-generation are ad hoc brainstorming techniques that encourage divergent thinking along some line of customer requirement – and not controlled convergence around developing new technologies that meet societal needs, articulated or not.

Therefore, conceptually based strategic development is mostly left to the machinations of a designer, engineer, or development team, and the best effort they can produce within some deadline given certain resource restraints. And although you need many of the psychological and emotional methods used by these groups, you also need a concept-development methodology that is robust, reliable, repeatable, and predictable based on scientific and empirical evaluation.

The idea is to ensure that your business, product, and process development is robust to the utmost extent, because everything you do from that point forward is an amplification of that initial work product. Therefore, if you're amplifying a low-value concept, your chances of generating high customer and shareholder value is minimal. If, on the other hand, you're amplifying a high-value concept, the outcome will be maximal within the natural constraints of the business.

22

The Cycle of Excellence

With all this as backdrop, let's take a holistic look at the TPE model. First, we said a grandly unified, integrated model of performance excellence is not only inevitable due to the unstoppable force of hybridizing evolution, but it's also happening right now. Second, we said that such a model is only a guide and not the Holy Grail of management. Third, we said that the model requires robustness and connectivity across the three dimensions of Strategy, Improvement, and Innovation. Fourth was the point that the elements of the model (tools and methods) get traction from an underlying progression of thought based on Axiomatic Design, and from our work in adding a fifth domain to Dr. Nam Suh's progression.

Fifth is the idea that all pieces of the TPE model have to be functioning optimally for the whole to function optimally, even though it can appear at times that one piece or set of pieces is more important to implement than others. This may be very true as an organization configures its strategic intent and responds to the political dictates of the quarter or operating year. But if you look at the TPE model as a water-faring vessel, you don't want it to have any big holes and, at a minimum, you want to understand how the parts effect the whole, and vice versa. (See Figure 20-2.)

In the best cases, an organization begins its Total Performance Excellence journey with Strategic Thinking, which entails envisioning the fuzzy edge of latent societal and customer need. At the same time the organization envisions such discontinuous change, it configures a view of continuous improvement to preserve and extend its current foothold in the marketplace. With a balanced picture of how the organization can preserve its current position, while also evolving into something different, it can derive great value from Strategic Planning methods, which connect strategy and execution as inseparable parts of a seamless whole.

Key outcomes of Strategic Thinking and Strategic Planning are focused vision, meaningful missions, prioritized goals, aligned objectives, rational metrics, optimized tactics, and systematic review cycles. This is the robust framework within which an organization can synergize otherwise disparate attempts to improve operations and innovate new value propositions.

With priorities and metrics defined and rationally deployed, the high-performing organization can use Process Management to define and operate its key, subordinate, and enabling processes, all of which are aligned with strategic direction. With a sound process architecture in place, Lean and Six Sigma methods are engaged to optimize performance from the standpoint of time and quality. In the language of TPE, these elements serve to preserve a company's position and success, because they enable an organization to optimize its current offerings, capabilities, technologies, and processes. Such optimization and constant improvement is a baseline requirement for keeping pace with the progressive nature of business.

Key outcomes of Process Management, Lean, and Six Sigma are operational stability, measurement integrity, reduced waste, minimized inventory, reduced variation, higher margins, increased capacity, reduced cycle time, lower costs, and other benefits, not the least of which is a culture of people relentlessly committed to improvement.

Although Strategic Thinking is a means for making the job of discontinuous change easier at the business level of an enterprise, Design for Six Sigma (DFSS) and TRIZ are used to create innovation at the operational and technical levels. Such ground-level innovation then dovetails with Strategic Thinking at the top and the cycle repeats itself.

> "Many business leaders spend vast amounts of time learning and promulgating the latest management techniques. But their failure to understand and practice execution negates the value of almost all they learn and preach. Such leaders are building houses without foundations."
>
> —————— Larry Bossidy

Former Chairman of IBM's Board Louis Gerstner once said that "strategy is execution," and this seems as true as it is outrageous. Then you have former CEO of Honeywell Larry Bossidy writing in his book, *Execution*, that "unless you translate big thoughts into concrete steps for action, they're pointless." And we know that both of these modern expressions are regurgitations of what Peter Drucker once said, "strategy must degenerate into work."

One thing's for sure about Drucker and the rest: They're striking a chord of truth that says a viable business needs a golden braid of connection between what it plans and what it does. Said another way, leadership and doer-ship go together like brain and hands, one playing off the other in an interdependent dynamism of dreams, realities, plans, actions, and adjustments that form the perpetual iteration of organizational identity.

Like the big hopes organizations have to be the best at what they do, we have a dream for how organizations can become the very best — where holistically passionate and robustly designed leadership is connected with holistically passionate and robustly designed doer-ship. If that all sounds the same, it should, because an organization is really one big connected family, and no one part should act in a way that doesn't serve the whole.

If you really think about it, the diseases of sub-optimization and waste in an organization build up over time as bad behavior and systems promulgate, just as poor health habits build up over time into stubbornly engrained symptoms. One must exert significant force to dislodge that inertia, which is why so many narrowly focused improvement initiatives fail to produce impressive results consistently. Although the investment is made in the tool (Lean for example), there is no investment in the structure for optimizing the way it, and other tools, are coordinated together.

> "... avoid Brewer's trap of misplaced optimization. Continue to improve your business process management capabilities, but don't intermix this goal with optimizing non-value-adding business processes."
> — Howard Smith and Peter Fingar, *Business Process Trends*, July 2004

Maybe organizations should be training TPE champions and practitioners in addition to training black belts, Kaizen event facilitators, TRIZ experts, risk managers, and so on. Yes, we know, the initial resistance is, "Oh no, not more people to train!" But the reality is that corporate skill sets have to — must — keep up with an evolving world. And in this evolving world, the force of leadership will have to make tangible steps toward performance excellence integration.

Therefore, we think it's wise for an organization to implement the parts of TPE that it can, with the vision of the whole in mind. Often, when an organization implements a powerful tool like Six Sigma, or a powerfully hybridized tool like Lean Sigma, the force of the initiative is strong enough to dislodge inertia, and the whole structure of performance begins to shift. Major operational improvements result in pressure on R&D to innovate the next product, which it does, which puts pressure on the strategy makers to think smarter about making a better world.

If all the gears and wheels of performance success are defined into an overarching model, an organization will know better how to sequence and direct its portfolio of interventions over time. As one initiative gains momentum and makes an impact, others are planned, because the effect of one program will dwindle as it bumps up against challenges it's not equipped to handle. Once you've pruned the tree into its ultimate state of beauty, you can't use that same tool to plant new trees. Once you've solved all the stubborn problems you have with Six Sigma, you can't use Six Sigma to make and manage a strategic plan.

Of course running a successful enterprise is a much larger task than any one program or initiative can handle. There has been enormous movement toward holism and consolidation in managerial know-how over the past 100 years, and this will continue by sheer force of evolution. It seems inevitable that the domains of Strategy, Improvement, and Innovation will come together even more over time as their methods connect and blend.

The reason TRIZ is so important is because it enables an organization to become truly innovative in formulating its strategic identity, and TRIZ pushes the minds of its leaders out onto the fuzzy edge of what they can become. At the corporate level, TRIZ is an engine for rational, structured, and historically proven idea generation. TRIZ, in concert with other strategic thinking tools, generates a set of data that changes the way organizations think and plan the future, and the way they connect strategy with execution.

Corporate leaders are certainly not willing to withstand a lengthy decision process when it comes to making strategy. And in the context of Total Performance Excellence, the core force of your vision, missions, and goals determines the impact of the many methods you implement to achieve them. TRIZ can fuel the development of robust Strategic Thinking. Then the methodologies of Strategic Planning, Process Management, Lean, Six Sigma, and DFSS, in some rational configuration, magnify that intent into reality. But TRIZ also drives innovation at the technical level, enabling discontinuous change to occur microscopically, project by project, function by function, process by process — even as it fuels change at the top.

The key to innovation is in making it more structured, predictable, measurable, and controllable. Once, the work of continuous improvement was envisioned and enacted by only a visionary few. Today, the drive to improve is known and practiced by all, because organizations figured out how to deploy and implement various methods for all to use. You are on that same edge today with the imperative to constantly innovate, and TRIZ is the methodology by which the job of innovation can become the job of all.

Part Four: Enveloping Total Performance

Business as Usual Versus Business as Exceptional

Business as Usual	Business as Exceptional
Isolated performance-improvement initiatives	Holistic performance-excellence framework
Achieve better or faster or cheaper	Achieve better and faster and cheaper
Method of the day	Grand Unification Theory of Business
Corporate Brownian Motion	Aligned strategic and tactical activity
Customer requirements as basis for innovation	Societal need as basis for innovation
Evolution by historical derivation	Evolution by intentional hybridization
Ad hoc adoption	Planned deployment
Fuzzy front end	Focused front end

Practical Advice

- Institute a total performance excellence framework at the leadership level of the organization.

- Drive, plan, and control multiple and separately focused (Improvement, Innovation) initiatives through the same managerial infrastructure.

- Institute a process whereby resources can be allocated to initiatives based on the balanced needs of the organization to preserve itself, while also innovating itself.

- Create a culture wherein different initiatives optimize rather than compete for resources.

- Intentionally identify unmet societal needs to drive product/process development.

- Align activity around common goals and subsidize the use of systematic innovation.

- Incorporate all necessary competencies into your business model so your practices are supported from mind to market.

Endnotes

36 Valentino, Dan, *Transformation*, Autumn, 1993, p. 29.

37 See O'Reilly III, Charles A, and Tushman, Michael L., "The Ambidextrous Organization," *Harvard Business Review*, 2004.

Appendix 1
The Economics of Innovation

You know from the field of psychology that behavior is a function of values, so an organization has to value innovation if it is to consistently engage in innovative behaviors. But what if your organization doesn't value innovation like it says it does? What if your organization is like so many that pay lip service to innovation — say they value it — yet don't consistently demonstrate the behaviors necessary to make innovation happen faster, more predictably, and more pervasively?

If you say you value the amount of money in your bank account, surely you have a way to measure and check up on that. This was the whole approach with Six Sigma related to the drive for operational improvement. Although most organizations once paid lip service to quality, Six Sigma forced them to measure quality as they never had before. As a result, they truly came to value quality, and they engaged in behaviors that brought about unprecedented levels of quality.

A Boston Consulting Group report cited in Part One calls for better innovation-related metrics and, surprisingly, points out that a sizeable 49 percent of corporate executives around the world do not carefully track the financial returns associated with each innovation. And seven percent say they aren't sure if their companies track innovation ROI at all. We believe this is a most telling phenomenon: Although most companies are dissatisfied with R&D results, most also don't know how they measure R&D ROI.

Still, trying to measure better isn't the whole answer, even though it's a great first step. In the 1980s an interesting business concept called "the cost of poor quality" drove a lot of activity around measuring poor quality and, naturally, improving quality. We're at a similar place today with innovation. Companies are beginning to measure the cost of poor innovation, and they're developing the systems for improving innovation ROI and traceability.

The following table gives a summarization of some metrics that could be used to track innovation success. It is not intended to be an exhaustive or universal list, but represents the ways in which companies should think.

The Economics of Innovation

Metric Category	Some Suggested Metrics
Macro	• Speed-to-change cultural bias • Amount of innovation budget • Ambidextrous index: balance of resource allocation between preservation and evolution (capital, human, technology) • Time to transition from preservation activity to evolution activity • Ratio of innovation projects sponsored by executives (disruptive technologies can't occur without senior management sponsorship)
Volume	• Number of innovations made • Number of invention disclosures • Number of patent applications filed • Number of trademarks obtained • Number of people involved in systematic problem solving • Number of systematic innovation projects completed • Variance of all the above
Speed	• Time to predict customer/market evolution • Amount of time per innovation • Research cycle time • Product development cycle time • Mean time to solve an innovation problem • Mean time to implement an innovation solution • Variance of all the above
Quality	• Ratio of innovations attempted to innovations made • Time to abandon a poor idea • Degree of discontinuity (level) • Costs avoided • New revenue generated • Costs reduced • Mean Ideality of innovation solutions • Variance of all the above

Appendix 2
The 76 Standard Solutions[38]

The 76 standard solutions are used to solve relatively common optimization problems. When appropriate, they can be applied in lieu of the innovation algorithm and its associated problem parameters and inventive principles. The 76 standard solutions are broken down into the following categories:

1) Improving the System with Little or No Change (13)

2) Improving the System by Changing the System (23)

3) System Transitions (6)

4) Detection and Measurement (17)

5) Strategies for Simplification and Improvement (17)

38 Salamatov, Yuri (edited by Souchkov, Valeri and technical editor, Slocum, Michael), *TRIZ: The Right Solution at the Right Time*, Insytec B.V., The Netherlands, 1999, pp. 226-244.

Improving the System with Little or No Change
(Standards 1-1-1 through 1-2-5)

STANDARD 1-1-1

If there is an object which is not easy to change as required, and the conditions do not contain any limitations on the introduction of substances and fields, the problem is to be solved by synthesizing a Substance Field Model (SFM): the object is subjected to the action of a physical field which produces the necessary change in the object.

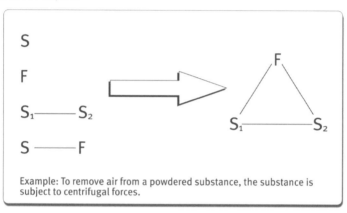

Example: To remove air from a powdered substance, the substance is subject to centrifugal forces.

STANDARD 1-1-2

If there is a SFM which is not easy to change as required, and the conditions do not contain any limitations on the introduction of additives to given substances, the problem is to be solved by a transition (permanent or temporary) to an internal complex SFM, introducing additives in the present substances enhancing controllability or imparting the required properties to the SFM.

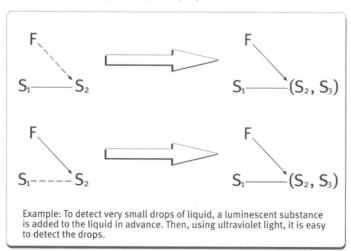

Example: To detect very small drops of liquid, a luminescent substance is added to the liquid in advance. Then, using ultraviolet light, it is easy to detect the drops.

STANDARD 1-1-3

If there is a SFM which is not easy to change as required, and the conditions contain limitations on the introduction of additives into the exiting substances, the problem can be solved by a transition (permanent or temporary) to an external complex SFM, attaching to one of these substances an external substance which improves controllability or brings the required properties to the SFM.

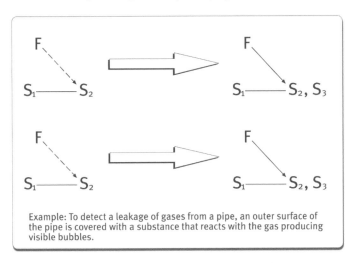

Example: To detect a leakage of gases from a pipe, an outer surface of the pipe is covered with a substance that reacts with the gas producing visible bubbles.

STANDARD 1-1-4

If there is a SFM that is not easy to change as required, and the conditions contain limitations on the introduction or attachment of substances, the problem has to be solved by synthesizing a SFM using external environment as the substance.

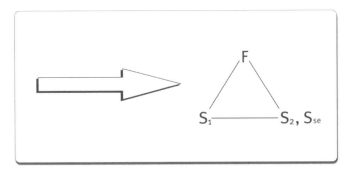

STANDARD 1-1-5

If the external environment does not contain ready substances required to synthesize a SFM, these substances can be obtained by replacing the external environment with another one, or by decomposing the environment, or by introducing additives into the environment.

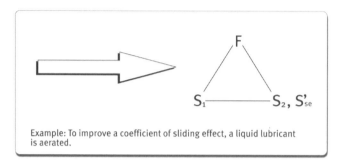

Example: To improve a coefficient of sliding effect, a liquid lubricant is aerated.

STANDARD 1-1-6

If a minimum (measured, optimal) effect of action is required, but it is difficult or impossible to provide it under the conditions of the problem, use a maximum action, while the excess of the action is then removed. Excess of a substance is removed by a field, while excess of a field is removed by a substance.

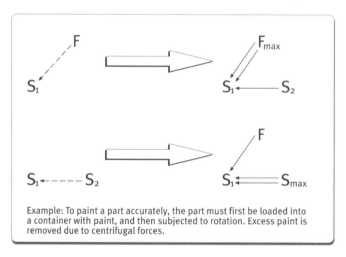

Example: To paint a part accurately, the part must first be loaded into a container with paint, and then subjected to rotation. Excess paint is removed due to centrifugal forces.

STANDARD 1-1-7

If a maximum effect of action on a substance is required and this is not allowed, the maximum action has to be preserved but directed to another substance attached to the first one.

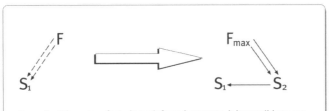

Example: When manufacturing reinforced concrete, it is possible to use metal wire instead of rods. But the wire has to be stretched. To do this it has to be heated to 700C which is not allowed. The wire is connected to the rod that is heated while the wire remains cold.

STANDARD 1-1-8-1

If a selective effect of action is required (maximum in certain zones, while the minimum is maintained in other zones), the field has to be maximal; then a protective substance is introduced in places where a minimum effect is required.

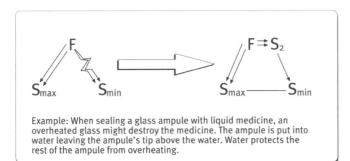

Example: When sealing a glass ampule with liquid medicine, an overheated glass might destroy the medicine. The ampule is put into water leaving the ampule's tip above the water. Water protects the rest of the ampule from overheating.

STANDARD 1-1-8-2

If a selective-maximum effect is required (maximum in certain zones, and minimum in other zones), the field should be minimal; then a substance that produces a local effect interacting with a field (e.g. termite compounds for thermal action or explosive ones for mechanical action) is introduced in places where a maximum effect is required.

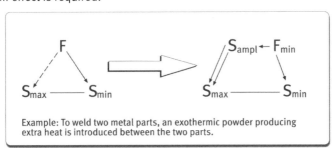

Example: To weld two metal parts, an exothermic powder producing extra heat is introduced between the two parts.

STANDARD 1-2-1

If useful and harmful effects appear between two substances in a SFM and there is no need to maintain a direct contact between the substances, the problem is solved by introducing a third substance between them.

Notes: The third substance can also be obtained from the present substances by exposure to the exiting fields. In particular, the substance to be introduced can be bubbles, foam, etc.

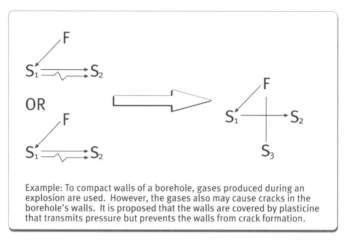

Example: To compact walls of a borehole, gases produced during an explosion are used. However, the gases also may cause cracks in the borehole's walls. It is proposed that the walls are covered by plasticine that transmits pressure but prevents the walls from crack formation.

STANDARD 1-2-2

If there are useful and a harmful effects between two substances, and there is no need to maintain direct contact between the substances, and it is forbidden or inconvenient to use foreign substances, the problem can be solved by introducing a third substance between the two, which is a modification of the first or the second substances.

Notes: The third substance can be obtained from the existing substances by exposure to the present fields. In particular, the substance to be introduced can be bubbles, foam, etc. Besides, a modification of the substance may bring about a change in the law of its movement: movable-fixed parts, etc.

$$S_1' \xrightarrow{F} S_2$$
$$S_1'(\text{or } S_2')$$

Example: A hydrodynamic foil's surface might be destroyed by a cavitation produced by the friction between the foil and the water when moving at a high speed. It is proposed to refrigerate the surface of the foil. Surrounding water will freeze and form an ice layer on the foil.

STANDARD 1-2-3

If it is required to eliminate the harmful effect of a field upon a substance, the problem can be solved by introducing a second substance that draws off upon itself the harmful effect of the field.

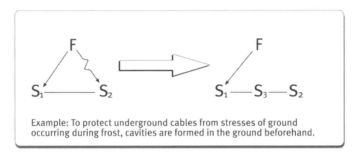

Example: To protect underground cables from stresses of ground occurring during frost, cavities are formed in the ground beforehand.

STANDARD 1-2-4

If useful and harmful effects appear between two substances in a SFM, and a direct contact between the substances must be maintained, the problem can be solved by transition to a dual SFM, in which the useful effect is provided by the existing field while a new field neutralizes the harmful effect (or transforms the harmful effect into a useful effect).

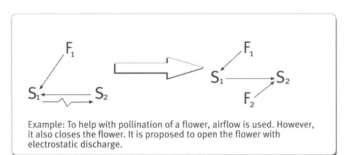

Example: To help with pollination of a flower, airflow is used. However, it also closes the flower. It is proposed to open the flower with electrostatic discharge.

STANDARD 1-2-5

If it is necessary to decompose a SFM with a magnetic field, the problem is solved by using physical effects, which are capable of "switching off" ferromagnetic properties of substances, e.g. by demagnetizing during an impact or during heating above Curie point.

Notes: The magnetic field may appear at the right moment if a system of magnets compensating the effect of each other's field is used. When one of the magnets is demagnetized, a magnetic field arises in the system.

Example: During welding, it is difficult to insert a ferromagnetic powder in the welding zone: an electromagnetic field of a welding current makes the particles move away from the welding zone. It is proposed to heat the powders above the Curie point to make them non-magnetic.

Improving the System by Changing the System
(Standards 2-1-1 through 2-4-12)

STANDARD 2-1-1

Efficiency of SFM can be improved by transforming one of the parts of the SFM into an independently controllable SFM, thus forming a chain SFM.

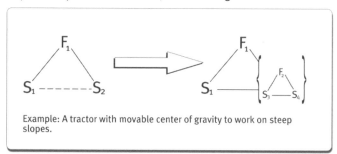

Example: A tractor with movable center of gravity to work on steep slopes.

STANDARD 2-1-2

If it is necessary to improve the efficiency of SFM, and replacement of SFM elements is not allowed, the problem can be solved by the synthesis of a dual SFM through introducing a second SFM, which is easy to control.

Example: It is proposed to increase control over a melted metal by rotating the metal in a centrifuge.

STANDARD 2-2-1

Efficiency of a SFM can be improved by replacing an uncontrolled (or poorly controlled) field with a well-controlled field, e.g. by replacing a gravitation field with a mechanical field, mechanical field with an electric, etc.

Notes: In certain situations, controllability of a field may be improved not only by replacing a given field with another one, but also by modifying the present field along the following line:

Permanent field → monotonically changing one → pulsed one → variable one → variable in frequency and amplitude → etc.

Example: Instead of a metal blade for non-uniform metal cutting, a water jet can be used.

STANDARD 2-2-2

Efficiency of a SFM can be improved by increasing the degree of fragmentation of the object, which acts as an instrument in SFM.

Notes: The standard displays one of the major trends of the technology evolution, i.e. fragmentation of the object or its part interacting with the product.

Example: A knife with teeth, then with the abrasive coating.

STANDARD 2-2-3

Efficiency of a SFM can be improved by transition from a solid object to a capillary porous one. The transition is performed as:

Solid object → object with one cavity → object with multiple cavities (perforated) → capillary porous object → capillary porous object with a predefined porous structure.

Notes: Transition to a capillary porous object enables a liquid substance to be placed in the pores and use physical effects.

Example: A bunch of capillaries apply liquid glue more accurately on a surface to be glued than a single large-sized tube.

STANDARD 2-2-4
Efficiency of a SFM can be improved by increasing the degree of dynamics of SFM, i.e. by transition to a more flexible, rapidly changing structure of the system.

Notes: Making a substance dynamic starts with dividing it into two joint-coupled parts and continues along the following line:

One joint → many joints → flexible object.

A field can be made more dynamic by transition from a permanent field (or of the field together with a substance) to a pulsed field.

Example: A door made a of hinged segments.

STANDARD 2-2-5
Efficiency of SFM can be improved by transition from a uniform field or fields with a disordered structure to non-uniform fields or fields with a definite spatial-temporal structure (permanent or variable).

Notes: If a certain spatial structure is to be imparted to a substance object, the process can be conducted in a field having a structure that matches the required structure of the substance object.

Example: To mix two magnetic powders, a layer of the first powder is put in the layer of the second powder and the non-uniform magnetic field is applied.

STANDARD 2-2-6
Efficiency of a SFM can be improved by transition from substances that are uniform or have a disordered structure to substances that are non-uniform or have a predefined spatial-temporal structure (permanent or variable).

Notes: In particular, if an intensive effect of a field is required in certain places of a system (points, lines), then substances that produce the required field are introduced in these spots beforehand.

Example: To make a porous material with oriented spatial structure, the field threats are inserted into the soft material beforehand. After the material solidifies these threats are burned out.

STANDARD 2-3-1
Efficiency of a SFM can be improved by matching (or mismatching) the frequency of acting field with the natural frequency of a product (or tool).

Example: The rhythm of massage is synchronized with a pulse of a patient.

Example: In arc welding, the frequency of magnetic field is equal to the natural frequency of a melting electrode.

STANDARD 2-3-2
Efficiency of a complex SFM can be improved by matching (or mismatching) frequencies of the fields being used.

Example: To coat a part with a material, the material is applied as a powder. To provide a high degree of regularity, the frequencies of pulses of an electrical current and pulses of magnetic field are made equal.

STANDARD 2-3-3
If we are given two incompatible actions, e.g. changing and measuring, one action should be performed during the pauses between another one. In general, pauses in one action should be filled by another useful action.

Example: To provide accuracy of contact welding, measurements are conducted during the pauses between the pulses of an electrical current.

STANDARD 2-4-1
Efficiency of a SFM is enhanced by using a ferromagnetic substance and a magnetic field.

Notes: The standard indicates the use of a ferromagnetic substance that is not in a fragmented state. F-SFM is a SFM system in which a disperse ferromagnetic substance and a magnetic field are interacting.

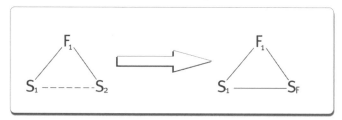

STANDARD 2-4-2
Efficiency of control over a SFM can be improved by replacing one of the substances with ferromagnetic particles (or adding ferromagnetic particles) – chips, granules, grains, etc. – and using magnetic or electromagnetic field.

Notes: Efficiency of control rises with a higher degree of fragmentation of ferromagnetic particles and of the substance in which they are introduced.

Ferro particles: granules → powder → finely dispersed particles → magnetic liquid;

Substance: solid → grains → powder → liquid

STANDARD 2-4-3
Efficiency of a ferromagnetic SFM can be improved by using magnetic fluids – colloidal ferromagnetic particles suspended in kerosene, silicone, or water.

STANDARD 2-4-4
Efficiency of a ferromagnetic SFM can be improved by using a capillary porous structure inherent in many F-SFMs.

STANDARD 2-4-5
If it is required to raise the efficiency of control and replacement of substances with ferromagnetic particles is not allowed, one has to compose internal or external complex ferromagnetic SFM, introducing additives in one of the substances.

STANDARD 2-4-6
If it is required to raise the efficiency of control and replacement of substances

with ferromagnetic particles is not allowed, the ferromagnetic particles should be introduced in the external environment. Then, using the magnetic field, the environment parameters should be changed so that the system becomes more controllable.

STANDARD 2-4-7
Controllability of a ferromagnetic system can be improved by the use of physical effects.

STANDARD 2-4-8
Efficiency of a F-SFM can be improved by increasing the degree of dynamics in the system, for instance, by transition to a more flexible, rapidly changing structure of the system.
Notes: Making a substance more dynamic begins with dividing it into two joint-coupled parts and continues along the following line:
One joint → many joints → flexible substance.
A field is made dynamic by going over from a permanent effect of the field (or of the field together with a substance) to a pulsed effect.

STANDARD 2-4-9
Efficiency of F-SFM can be improved by transition from fields that are uniform or have a disordered structure to fields that are non-uniform or have a definite spatial-temporal structure (permanent or variable).
Notes: If a certain spatial structure is to be imparted to a substance object, the process can be conducted in a field having a structure that matches the required structure of the substance object.

STANDARD 2-4-10
Efficiency of F-SFM can be improved by matching the rhythms of the system's elements.

STANDARD 2-4-11
If it is not allowed to introduce ferromagnetics or to perform magnetization, an E-SFM has to be synthesized using: a) interaction of an external electromagnetic field with currents or b) fed through a contact or induced without a contact, or c) using interaction between these currents.
Notes: An E-SFM is a SFM in which electric currents interact with each other. The evolution of E-SFMs repeats the line of evolution of complex-boosted SFMs:
Simple E-SFM → complex E-SFM → E-SFM in the external environment → E-SFM Dynamization → structuring → matching the rhythms.

STANDARD 2-4-12
If a magnetic fluid cannot be used, one can use an electroheologic fluid (a suspension of fine quartz powder in toluene, for instance, with viscosity being changed by the electric field). A SFM with an electroheologic fluid is a special form of E-SFM.

System Transitions
(Standards 3-1-1 through 3-2-1)

STANDARD 3-1-1

System efficiency at any stage of its evolution can be improved by combining the system with another system (or systems) to form a bi- or poly-system.

Notes: For a simple formation of bi- and poly-systems, two and more components are combined. Components to be combined may be substances, fields, substance-field pairs, and whole SFMs.

Example: To process sides of thin glass plates, several plates are put together to prevent glass from breaking.

STANDARD 3-1-2

Efficiency of bi- and poly-systems can be improved by developing links between system elements.

Notes: Links between elements of a bi- and poly-system may be made either more rigid or more dynamic.

Example: To synchronize a process of lifting a very heavy part by three cranes, it is proposed to use a rigid triangle synchronizing the crane's moving parts.

STANDARD 3-1-3

Efficiency of bi- and poly-systems can be improved by increasing the difference between system components. The following line of evolution is recommended:

Similar components (pencils of the same color) → components with biased characteristics (pencils of different colors) → different components (set of drawing instruments) → combinations of the "component + component with opposite function" (pencil with rubber).

STANDARD 3-1-4

Efficiency of bi- and poly-systems can be improved by "convolution" (integration of several components into a single component) by reducing auxiliary components. Completely convoluted bi- and poly-systems become mono-systems again, and integration can be repeated at another level of the system.

Example: Instead of three separate indicators on a dashboard, a single indicator can be used in which indicating arrows are made of different colors.

STANDARD 3-1-5

Efficiency of bi- and poly-systems can be improved by distributing incompatible properties among the system and its parts. This is achieved by using a two-level structure in which all the system as a whole has a certain property A, while its parts (particles) have property anti-A.

Example: A working part of a vice is made of segmented plates capable of moving relative to each other. Parts of various shapes can be gripped quickly.

STANDARD 3-2-1

Efficiency of a system at any stage of its evolution can be improved by transition from a macro level to a micro level: the system or its part is replaced by a substance capable of delivering the required function when interacting with a field.

Notes: There is a multitude of micro level states of a substance (crystal lattice, molecules, ions, domains, atoms, fundamental particles, fields, etc.). Therefore, various options of transition to a micro level and various options of transition from one micro level to another, lower one, should be considered when solving a problem.

Example: Instead of a micro-screw, a microscopic table can be positioned by fixing it on a metal rod that is subjected to a thermal field. The rod expands and contracts relative to the value of the temperature due to the effect of thermal expansion.

Detection and Measurement
(Standards 4-1-1 through 4-5-2)

STANDARD 4-1-1

If a problem involves detection or measurement, it is proposed to change the problem in such a way, so that there should be no need to perform detection of measurement at all.

Example: To prevent a permanent electric motor from overheating, its temperature is measured by a temperature sensor. If to make the poles of the motor of an alloy with a Curie point equal to the critical value of the temperature, the motor will stop itself.

STANDARD 4-1-2

If a problem involves detection of measurement, and it is impossible to change the problem to eliminate the need for detection or measurement, it is proposed to change/detect properties of a copy of the object (e.g. picture).

Example: It might be dangerous to measure the length of a snake. It is safe to measure its length on a photographic image of the snake, and then recalculate the obtained result.

STANDARD 4-1-3

If a problem involves detection or measurement, and the problem cannot be changed to eliminate the need for measurement, and it is impossible to use copies or pictures, it is proposed to transform this problem into a problem of successive detection of changes.

Notes: Any measurement is conducted with a certain degree of accuracy. Therefore, even if the problem deals with continuous measurement, one can always single out a simple act of measurement that involves two successive detections. This makes the problem much simpler.

Example: To measure a temperature, it is possible to use a material that changes its color depending on the current value of the temperature. Alternatively, several materials can be used to indicate different temperatures.

STANDARD 4-2-1

If a non-SFM is not easy to detect or measure, the problem is solved by synthesizing a simple or dual SFM with a field at the output. Instead of direct measurement or detection of a parameter, another parameter identified with the field is measured or detected. The field to be introduced should have a parameter that we can easily detect or measure, and which can indicate the state of the parameter we need to detect or measure.

STANDARD 4-2-2

If a system (or its part) does not provide detection or measurement, the problem is solved by transition to an internal or external complex measuring SFM, introducing easily detectable additives.

STANDARD 4-2-3

If a system is difficult to detect or to measure at a given moment of time, and it is not allowed or not possible to introduce additives into the object, then additives that create an easily detectable and measurable field should be introduced in the external environment. Changing the state of the environment will indicate the state of the object.

Example: To detect wearing of a rotating metal disc contacting with another disc, it is proposed to introduce luminescent powder into the oil lubricant, which already exists in the system. Metal particles collecting in the oil will reduce luminosity of the oil.

STANDARD 4-2-4

If it is impossible to introduce easily detectable additives in the external environment, these can be obtained in the environment itself, for instance, by decomposing the environment or by changing the aggregate state of the environment.

Notes: In particular, gas or vapor bubbles produced by electrolysis, cavitation, or by any other method may often be used as additives obtained by decomposing the external environment.

Example: The speed of a water flow in a pipe might be measured by the amount of air bubbles resulting from cavitation.

STANDARD 4-3-1

Efficiency of measuring SFM can be improved by the use of physical effects.

Example: Temperature of liquid media can be measured by measuring a change of a coefficient of retraction, which depends on the value of the temperature.

STANDARD 4-3-2

If it is impossible to detect or measure directly the changes in the system, and no field can be passed through the system, the problem can be solved by exciting resonance oscillations (of the entire system or of its part), whose frequency change is an indication of the changes taking place.

Example: To measure the mass of a substance in a container, the container is subjected to mechanically forced resonance oscillations. The frequency of the oscillations depends on the mass of the system.

STANDARD 4-3-3

If resonance oscillations may not be excited in a system, its state can be determined by a change in the natural frequency of the object (external environment) connected with the system.

Example: The mass of boiling liquid can be measured by measuring the natural frequency of gas resulting form evaporation.

STANDARD 4-4-1

Efficiency of a measuring SFM can be improved by using a ferromagnetic substance and a magnetic field.

Notes: The standard indicates the use of a non-fragmented ferromagnetic object.

STANDARD 4-4-2

Efficiency of detection or measurement can be improved by transition to ferromagnetic SFMs, replacing one of the substances with ferromagnetic particles (or adding ferromagnetic particles) and by detecting or measuring the magnetic field.

STANDARD 4-4-3

If it is required to improve the efficiency of detection or measurement by transition to a ferromagnetic SFM, and replacement of the substance with ferromagnetic particles is not allowed, the transition to the F-SFM is performed by synthesizing a complex ferromagnetic SFM, introducing (or attaching) ferromagnetic additives in the substance.

STANDARD 4-4-4

If it is required to improve efficiency of detection or measurement by transition to F-SFM, and introduction of ferromagnetic particles is not allowed, ferromagnetic particles are introduced in the external environment.

STANDARD 4-4-5

Efficiency of a F-SFM measuring system can be improved by using physical effects, for instance, Curie point, Hopkins and Barkhausen effects, magneto-elastic effect, etc.

STANDARD 4-5-1

Efficiency of a measuring system at any stage of its evolution can be improved by forming bi- and poly-system.

Notes: To form bi- and poly-systems, two or more components are combined. The components to be combined may be substances, fields, substance-field pairs, and SFMs.

Example: It is difficult to accurately measure the temperature of a small beetle. However, if there are many beetles put together, the temperature can be measured easily.

STANDARD 4-5-2

Measuring systems evolve towards measuring the derivatives of the function under control. The transition is performed along the following line:

Measurement of a function → measurement of the first derivative of the function → measurement of the second derivative of the function.

Example: Change of stress in the rock is defined by the speed of changing the electrical resistance of the rock.

Strategies for Simplification and Improvement
(Standards 5-1-1-1 through 5-5-3)

STANDARD 5-1-1-1

If it is necessary to introduce a substance in the system, and it is not allowed, a "void" can be used instead of the substance.

Notes: A "void" is usually gaseous substance, like air, or empty space formed in a solid object. In some cases a "void" may be formed by other substances such as liquids (foam) or loose bodies.

STANDARD 5-1-1-2

If it is necessary to introduce a substance in the system, and it is not allowed, a field can be introduced instead of the substance.

STANDARD 5-1-1-3

If it is necessary to introduce a substance in the system, and it is not allowed, an external additive can be used instead of an internal one.

STANDARD 5-1-1-4

If it is necessary to introduce a substance in the system, and it is not allowed, a very active additive can be introduced in very small quantities.

STANDARD 5-1-1-5

If it is necessary to introduce a substance in the system, and it is not allowed, an additive can be introduced in very small quantities and concentrated in certain parts of the object.

STANDARD 5-1-1-6

If it is necessary to introduce a substance in the system, and it is not allowed, the substance can be introduced temporarily and then removed.

STANDARD 5-1-1-7

If it is necessary to introduce a substance in the system, and it is not allowed, a copy of the object can be used instead of the object itself, where introduction of substances is allowed.

STANDARD 5-1-1-8

If it is necessary to introduce a substance in the system, and it is not allowed by the system's operating conditions, the substance can be introduced in a form of a chemical compound, which can be later decomposed.

STANDARD 5-1-1-9

If it is necessary to introduce a substance in the system, and it is not allowed, the substance can be produced by decomposing the external environment or the object itself, for instance, by electrolysis, or by changing the aggregate state of a part of the object or external environment.

STANDARD 5-1-2

If a system is not easy to change as required, and the conditions do not allow to replace the component acting as an instrument or introduce additives, the artifact has to be used instead of the instrument, dividing the artifact into parts interacting with each other.

STANDARD 5-1-3

After the substance introduced in the system has fulfilled its function, it should either disappear or become indistinguishable from the substance that was in the system or in the external environment before.

Notes: The substance that has been introduced may disappear due to chemical reactions or change of phase.

STANDARD 5-1-4

If it is necessary to introduce a large quantity of a substance, but this is not allowed, a "void" in the form of inflatable structures or foam should be used as the substance.

Notes: Introduction of foam or inflatable structures resolves a contradiction 'much substance – little substance'.

STANDARD 5-2-1

If a field has to be introduced in a SFM, one should use first of all the present fields for which the media are those substances that form the system or its part.

Notes: The use of substances and fields, which already present in the system, improves the system's ideality: number of functions performed by the system increases without increasing the number of used components.

STANDARD 5-2-2

If a field has to be introduced in a SFM and it is not possible to use the fields, which already present in the system, one should use the fields of the external environment.

Notes: The use of external environment fields (gravitation, thermal field, pressure...) improves the system's ideality: the number of functions performed by the system increases without increasing the number of used components.

STANDARD 5-2-3

If a field has to be introduced in a SFM but it is impossible to use the fields, which already present in the system or in the external environment, one should use the fields for which the substances present in the system or external environment can act as media or sources.

Notes: In particular, if there are ferromagnetic substances in a system and they are used for mechanical purposes, it is possible to use their magnetic properties in order to obtain additional effects: improve interactions between components, obtain information on the state of the system, etc.

STANDARD 5-3-1

Efficiency of the use of a substance without introducing other substances can be improved by changing its phase.

STANDARD 5-3-2

"Dual" properties are provided by using substances capable of converting from one phase to another according to operating conditions.

STANDARD 5-3-3

Efficiency of a system can be improved by the use of physical phenomena accompanying a phase transition.

Notes: Structure of a substance, density, thermal conductivity, etc. also changes along with the change of aggregate state during all types of phase transitions. In addition, during phase transitions, energy may be released or absorbed.

STANDARD 5-3-4

"Dual" properties of a system are provided by replacing a single-phase state of the substance with a dual-phase state.

STANDARD 5-3-5

Efficiency of systems obtained as a result of replacing a substance's single-phase state with a dual-phase state can be improved by introducing interaction (physical or chemical) between parts (phases) of the system.

STANDARD 5-4-1

If an object is to be alternating between different physical states, the transition is performed by the object, itself using reversible physical transformations, e.g. phase transitions, ionization-recombination, dissociation-association, etc.

Notes: A dynamic balance providing for the process self-adjustment or stabilization may be maintained in the dual-phase state.

STANDARD 5-4-2

If it is necessary to obtain a strong effect at the system's output, given a weak effect at the input, the transformer substance is placed to a condition close to critical. The energy is stored in the substance, and the input signal acts as a "trigger."

STANDARD 5-5-1

If substance particles (e.g. ions) are required to solve a problem and they are not available according to the problem conditions, the required particles can be obtained by decomposing a substance of a higher structural level (e.g. molecules).

STANDARD 5-5-2

If substance particles (e.g. molecules) are required to solve a problem and they cannot be produced by decomposing a substance of a higher structural level, the required particles can be obtained by combining particles of a lower structural level (e.g. ions).

STANDARD 5-5-3

If a substance of a higher structural level has to be decomposed, the easiest way is to decompose the nearest higher element. When combining particles of a lower structural level, the easiest way is to complete the nearest lower element.

Appendix 3
The 39 Problem Parameters[39]

The 39 problem parameters are used to aid analogical thinking when moving from a specific problem to a generic problem with the innovation algorithm. They are also used to converge on the inventive principles that are needed to resolve a given technical contradiction.

1. **Weight of moving object**
   The mass of the object, in a gravitational field. The force that the body exerts on its support or suspension.

2. **Weight of stationary object**
   The mass of the object, in a gravitational field. The force that the body exerts on its support or suspension, or on the surface on which it rests.

3. **Length of moving object**
   Any one linear dimension, not necessarily the longest, is considered a length.

4. **Length of stationary object**
   Same.

5. **Area of moving object**
   A geometrical characteristic described by the part of a plane enclosed by a line. The part of a surface occupied by the object. OR the square measure of the surface, either internal or external, of an object.

6. **Area of stationary object**
   Same.

7. **Volume of moving object**
   The cubic measure of space occupied by the object. Length x width x height for a rectangular object, height x area for a cylinder, etc.

8. **Volume of stationary object**
   Same.

9. **Speed**
   The velocity of an object; the rate of a process or action in time.

10. **Force**
    Force measures the interaction between systems. In Newtonian physics,

force = mass X acceleration. In TRIZ, force is any interaction that is intended to change an object's condition.

11. Stress or pressure
Force per unit area. Also, tension.

12. Shape
The external contours, appearance of a system.

13. Stability of the object's composition
The wholeness or integrity of the system; the relationship of the system's constituent elements. Wear, chemical decomposition, and disassembly all decrease instability. Increasing entropy is decreasing stability.

14. Strength
The extent to which the object is able to resist changing in response to force. Resistance to breaking.

15. Duration of action by a moving object
The time that the object can perform the action. Service life. Mean time between failure is a measure of the duration of action. Also, durability.

16. Duration of action by a stationary object
Same.

17. Temperature
The thermal condition of the object or system. Loosely includes other thermal parameters, such as heat capacity, that affect the rate of change of temperature.

18. Illumination intensity
Light flux per unit area. Also any other illumination characteristics of the system such as brightness, light quality, etc.

19. Use of energy by moving object
The measure of the object's capacity for doing work. In classical mechanics, Energy is the product of force times distance. This includes the use of energy provided by the super-system (such as electrical energy or heat.) Energy required to do a particular job.

20. Use of energy by stationary object
Same.

21. Power
The time rate at which work is performed. The rate of use of energy.

22. Loss of Energy
Use of energy that does not contribute to the job being done. See 19. Reducing the loss of energy sometimes requires different techniques from improving the use of energy, which is why this is a separate category.

23. Loss of substance
Partial or complete, permanent or temporary, loss of some of a system's materials, substances, parts, or subsystems.

24. Loss of Information
Partial or complete, permanent or temporary, loss of data or access to data in or by a system. Frequently includes sensory data such as aroma, texture, etc.

25. Loss of Time
Time is the duration of an activity. Improving the loss of time means reducing the time taken for the activity. "Cycle time reduction" is a common term.

26. Quantity of substance/the matter
The number or amount of a system's materials, substances, parts or subsystems which might be changed fully or partially, permanently or temporarily.

27. Reliability
A system's ability to perform its intended functions in predictable ways and conditions.

28. Measurement accuracy
The closeness of the measured value to the actual value of a property of a system. Reducing the error in a measurement increases the accuracy of the measurement.

29. Manufacturing precision
The extent to which the actual characteristics of the system or object match the specified or required characteristics.

30. External harm affects the object
Susceptibility of a system to externally generated (harmful) effects.

31. Object-generated harmful factors
A harmful effect is one that reduces the efficiency or quality of the functioning of the object or system. These harmful effects are generated by the object or system, as part of its operation.

32. Ease of manufacture
The degree of facility, comfort, or effortlessness in manufacturing or fabricating the object/system.

33. Ease of operation

Simplicity: The process is NOT easy if it requires a large number of people, large number of steps in the operation, needs special tools, etc. "Hard" processes have low yield and "easy" process have high yield; they are easy to do right.

34. Ease of repair

Quality characteristics such as convenience, comfort, simplicity, and time to repair faults, failures, or defects in a system.

35. Adaptability or versatility

The extent to which a system/object positively responds to external changes. Also, a system that can be used in multiple ways under a variety of circumstances.

36. Device complexity

The number and diversity of elements and element interrelationships within a system. The user may be an element of the system that increases the complexity. The difficulty of mastering the system is a measure of its complexity.

37. Difficulty of detecting and measuring

Measuring or monitoring systems that are complex, costly, require much time and labor to set up and use, or that have complex relationships between components or components that interfere with each other all demonstrate "difficulty of detecting and measuring." Increasing cost of measuring to a satisfactory error is also a sign of increased difficulty of measuring.

38. Extent of automation

The extent to which a system or object performs its functions without human interface. The lowest level of automation is the use of a manually operated tool. For intermediate levels, humans program the tool, observe its operation, and interrupt or re-program as needed. For the highest level, the machine senses the operation needed, programs itself, and monitors its own operations.

39. Productivity

The number of functions or operations performed by a system per unit time. The time for a unit function or operation. The output per unit time, or the cost per unit output.

39 Domb, E., Miller, J., MacGran, E., Slocum, M., "The 39 Features of Altshullers Contradiction Matrix." *The TRIZ Journal,* November, 1998, http://www.triz-journal.com.

Appendix 4
The 40 Inventive Principles[40]

The 40 inventive principles are the total set of generic solutions that populate the contradiction matrix. They are used to narrow the field of possible solutions to a given technical contradiction.

Principle 1. Segmentation
Divide an object into independent parts.
- Replace mainframe computer by personal computers.
- Replace a large truck by a truck and trailer.
- Use a work breakdown structure for a large project.

Make an object easy to disassemble.
- Modular furniture.
- Quick disconnect joints in plumbing.

Increase the degree of fragmentation or segmentation.
- Replace solid shades with Venetian blinds.
- Use powdered welding metal instead of foil or rod to get better penetration of the joint.

Principle 2. Taking out
Separate an interfering part or property from an object, or single out the only necessary part (or property) of an object.
- Locate a noisy compressor outside the building where compressed air is used.
- Use fiber optics or a light pipe to separate the hot light source from the location where light is needed.
- Use the sound of a barking dog, without the dog, as a burglar alarm.

Principle 3. Local quality
Change an object's structure from uniform to non-uniform, change an external environment (or external influence) from uniform to non-uniform.
- Use a temperature, density, or pressure gradient instead of constant temperature, density, or pressure.

Make each part of an object function in conditions most suitable for its operation.
- Lunch box with special compartments for hot and cold solid foods and for liquids.

Make each part of an object fulfill a different and useful function.
- Pencil with eraser.
- Hammer with nail puller.
- Multi-function tool that scales fish, acts as a pliers, a wire stripper, a flat-blade screwdriver, a Phillips screwdriver, manicure set, etc.

Principle 4. Asymmetry

Change the shape of an object from symmetrical to asymmetrical.

- Asymmetrical mixing vessels or asymmetrical vanes in symmetrical vessels improve mixing (cement trucks, cake mixers, blenders).
- Put a flat spot on a cylindrical shaft to attach a knob securely.

If an object is asymmetrical, increase its degree of asymmetry.

- Change from circular O-rings to oval cross-section to specialized shapes to improve sealing.
- Use astigmatic optics to merge colors.

Principle 5. Merging

Bring closer together (or merge) identical or similar objects, assemble identical or similar parts to perform parallel operations.

- Personal computers in a network.
- Thousands of microprocessors in a parallel processor computer.
- Vanes in a ventilation system.
- Electronic chips mounted on both sides of a circuit board or subassembly.

Make operations contiguous or parallel; bring them together in time.

- Link slats together in Venetian or vertical blinds.
- Medical diagnostic instruments that analyze multiple blood parameters simultaneously.
- Mulching lawnmower.

Principle 6. Universality

Make a part or object perform multiple functions; eliminate the need for other parts.

- Handle of a toothbrush contains toothpaste.
- Child's car safety seat converts to a stroller.
- Mulching lawnmower (Yes, it demonstrates both Principles 5 and 6, Merging and Universality.)
- Team leader acts as recorder and timekeeper.
- CCD (Charge coupled device) with micro-lenses formed on the surface.

Principle 7. "Nested doll"

Place one object inside another; place each object, in turn, inside the other.

- Measuring cups or spoons.
- Russian dolls.
- Portable audio system (microphone fits inside transmitter, which fits inside amplifier case).

Make one part pass through a cavity in the other.

- Extending radio antenna.
- Extending pointer.
- Zoom lens.
- Seat belt retraction mechanism.
- Retractable aircraft landing gear stow inside the fuselage (also demonstrates Principle 15, Dynamism).

Principle 8. Anti-weight
To compensate for the weight of an object, merge it with other objects that provide lift.
- Inject foaming agent into a bundle of logs, to make it float better.
- Use helium balloon to support advertising signs.

To compensate for the weight of an object, make it interact with the environment (e.g. use aerodynamic, hydrodynamic, buoyancy, and other forces).
- Aircraft wing shape reduces air density above the wing, increases density below wing, to create lift. (This also demonstrates Principle 4, Asymmetry.)
- Vortex strips improve lift of aircraft wings.
- Hydrofoils lift ship out of the water to reduce drag.

Principle 9. Preliminary anti-action
If it will be necessary to do an action with both harmful and useful effects, this action should be replaced with anti-actions to control harmful effects.
- Buffer a solution to prevent harm from extremes of pH.

Create beforehand stresses in an object that will oppose known undesirable working stresses later on.
- Pre-stress rebar before pouring concrete.
- Masking anything before harmful exposure: Use a lead apron on parts of the body not being exposed to X-rays. Use masking tape to protect the part of an object not being painted.

Principle 10. Preliminary action
Perform, before it is needed, the required change of an object (either fully or partially).
- Pre-pasted wall paper.
- Sterilize all instruments needed for a surgical procedure on a sealed tray.

Pre-arrange objects such that they can come into action from the most convenient place and without losing time for their delivery.
- Kanban arrangements in a Just-In-Time factory.
- Flexible manufacturing cell.

Principle 11. Beforehand cushioning
Prepare emergency means beforehand to compensate for the relatively low reliability of an object.
- Magnetic strip on photographic film that directs the developer to compensate for poor exposure.
- Back-up parachute.
- Alternate air system for aircraft instruments.

Principle 12. Equipotentiality
In a potential field, limit position changes (e.g. change operating conditions to eliminate the need to raise or lower objects in a gravity field).
- Spring loaded parts delivery system in a factory.
- Locks in a channel between two bodies of water (Panama Canal).
- "Skillets" in an automobile plant that bring all tools to the right position

(also demonstrates Principle 10, Preliminary Action).

Principle 13. 'The other way round'

Invert the action(s) used to solve the problem (e.g. instead of cooling an object, heat it).

- To loosen stuck parts, cool the inner part instead of heating the outer part.
- Bring the mountain to Mohammed, instead of bringing Mohammed to the mountain.

Make movable parts (or the external environment) fixed, and fixed parts movable.

- Rotate the part instead of the tool.
- Moving sidewalk with standing people.
- Treadmill (for walking or running in place).

Turn the object (or process) 'upside down.'

- Turn an assembly upside down to insert fasteners (especially screws).
- Empty grain from containers (ship or railroad) by inverting them.

Principle 14. Spheroidality - Curvature

Instead of using rectilinear parts, surfaces, or forms, use curvilinear ones; move from flat surfaces to spherical ones; from parts shaped as a cube (parallelepi ped) to ball-shaped structures.

- Use arches and domes for strength in architecture.

Use rollers, balls, spirals, domes.

- Spiral gear (Nautilus) produces continuous resistance for weight lifting.
- Ball point and roller point pens for smooth ink distribution.

Go from linear to rotary motion, use centrifugal forces.

- Produce linear motion of the cursor on the computer screen using a mouse or a trackball.
- Replace wringing clothes to remove water with spinning clothes in a washing machine.
- Use spherical casters instead of cylindrical wheels to move furniture.

Principle 15. Dynamics

Allow (or design) the characteristics of an object, external environment, or process to change to be optimal or to find an optimal operating condition.

- Adjustable steering wheel (or seat, or back support, or mirror position...)

Divide an object into parts capable of movement relative to each other.

- The "butterfly" computer keyboard (also demonstrates Principle 7, "Nested doll").

If an object (or process) is rigid or inflexible, make it movable or adaptive.

- The flexible boroscope for examining engines.
- The flexible sigmoidoscope, for medical examination.

Principle 16. Partial or excessive actions

If 100 percent of an object is hard to achieve using a given solution method then, by using 'slightly less' or 'slightly more' of the same method, the problem may be considerably easier to solve.

- Over spray when painting, then remove excess. (Or, use a stencil-this is an application of Principle 3, Local Quality and Principle 9, Preliminary anti-action).
- Fill, then "top off" when filling the gas tank of your car.

Principle 17. Another dimension
To move an object in two- or three-dimensional space.
- Infrared computer mouse moves in space, instead of on a surface, for presentations.
- Five-axis cutting tool can be positioned where needed.

Use a multi-story arrangement of objects instead of a single-story arrangement.
- Cassette with 6 CD's to increase music time and variety.
- Electronic chips on both sides of a printed circuit board.
- Employees "disappear" from the customers in a theme park, descend into a tunnel, and walk to their next assignment, where they return to the surface and magically reappear.

Tilt or re-orient the object, lay it on its side.
- Dump truck.

Use 'another side' of a given area.
- Stack microelectronic hybrid circuits to improve density.

Principle 18. Mechanical vibration
Cause an object to oscillate or vibrate.
- Electric carving knife with vibrating blades.

Increase its frequency (even up to the ultrasonic).
- Distribute powder with vibration.

Use an object's resonant frequency.
- Destroy gall stones or kidney stones using ultrasonic resonance.

Use piezoelectric vibrators instead of mechanical ones.
- Quartz crystal oscillations drive high accuracy clocks.

Use combined ultrasonic and electromagnetic field oscillations.
- Mixing alloys in an induction furnace.

Principle 19. Periodic action
Instead of continuous action, use periodic or pulsating actions.
- Hitting something repeatedly with a hammer.
- Replace a continuous siren with a pulsed sound.

If an action is already periodic, change the periodic magnitude or frequency.
- Use Frequency Modulation to convey information, instead of Morse code.
- Replace a continuous siren with sound that changes amplitude and frequency.

Use pauses between impulses to perform a different action.
- In cardio-pulmonary respiration (CPR), breathe after every five chest compressions.

Principle 20. Continuity of useful action

Carry on work continuously; make all parts of an object work at full load, all the time.

- Flywheel (or hydraulic system) stores energy when a vehicle stops, so the motor can keep running at optimum power.
- Run the bottleneck operations in a factory continuously, to reach the optimum pace. (From theory of constraints, or takt time operations)

Eliminate all idle or intermittent actions or work.

- Print during the return of a printer carriage-dot matrix printer, daisy wheel printers, inkjet printers.

Principle 21. Skipping

Conduct a process, or certain stages (e.g. destructible, harmful, or hazardous operations) at high speed.

- Use a high speed dentist's drill to avoid heating tissue.
- Cut plastic faster than heat can propagate in the material, to avoid deform ing the shape.

Principle 22. "Blessing in disguise" or "Turn lemons into lemonade"

Use harmful factors (particularly, harmful effects of the environment or surroundings) to achieve a positive effect.

- Use waste heat to generate electric power.
- Recycle waste (scrap) material from one process as raw materials for another.

Eliminate the primary harmful action by adding it to another harmful action to resolve the problem.

- Add a buffering material to a corrosive solution.
- Use a helium-oxygen mix for diving, to eliminate both nitrogen narcosis and oxygen poisoning from air and other nitrox mixes.

Amplify a harmful factor to such a degree that it is no longer harmful.

- Use a backfire to eliminate the fuel from a forest fire.

Principle 23. Feedback

Introduce feedback (referring back, cross-checking) to improve a process or action.

- Automatic volume control in audio circuits.
- Signal from gyrocompass is used to control simple aircraft autopilots.
- Statistical Process Control (SPC)-Measurements are used to decide when to modify a process. (Not all feedback systems are automated!)
- Budgets-Measurements are used to decide when to modify a process.

If feedback is already used, change its magnitude or influence.

- Change sensitivity of an autopilot when within five miles of an airport.
- Change sensitivity of a thermostat when cooling vs. heating, since it uses energy less efficiently when cooling.
- Change a management measure from budget variance to customer satisfaction.

Principle 24. 'Intermediary'

Use an intermediary carrier article or intermediary process.
- Carpenter's nail set, used between the hammer and the nail.

Merge one object temporarily with another (which can be easily removed).
- Pot holder to carry hot dishes to the table.

Principle 25. Self-service

Make an object serve itself by performing auxiliary helpful functions.
- A soda fountain pump that runs on the pressure of the carbon dioxide that is used to "fizz" the drinks. This assures that drinks will not be flat, and eliminates the need for sensors.
- Halogen lamps regenerate the filament during use-evaporated material is redeposited.
- To weld steel to aluminum, create an interface from alternating thin strips of the two materials. Cold weld the surface into a single unit with steel on one face and copper on the other, then use normal welding techniques to attach the steel object to the interface and the interface to the aluminum. (This concept also has elements of Principle 24, Intermediary, and Principle 4, Asymmetry.)

Use waste resources, energy, or substances.
- Use heat from a process to generate electricity: "Co-generation".
- Use animal waste as fertilizer.
- Use food and lawn waste to create compost.

Principle 26. Copying

Instead of an unavailable, expensive, fragile object, use simpler and inexpensive copies.
- Virtual reality via computer instead of an expensive vacation.
- Listen to an audio tape instead of attending a seminar.

Replace an object, or process with optical copies.
- Do surveying from space photographs instead of on the ground.
- Measure an object by measuring the photograph.
- Make sonograms to evaluate the health of a fetus, instead of risking damage by direct testing.

If visible optical copies are already used, move to infrared or ultraviolet copies.
- Make images in infrared to detect heat sources, such as diseases in crops, or intruders in a security system.

Principle 27. Cheap short-living objects

Replace an inexpensive object with a multiple of inexpensive objects, comprising certain qualities (such as service life, for instance).
- Use disposable paper objects to avoid the cost of cleaning and storing durable objects. Plastic cups in motels, disposable diapers, many kinds of medical supplies.

Principle 28. Mechanics substitution

Replace a mechanical means with a sensory (optical, acoustic, taste, or smell) means.

- Replace a physical fence to confine a dog or cat with an acoustic "fence" (signal audible to the animal).
- Use a bad-smelling compound in natural gas to alert users to leakage, instead of a mechanical or electrical sensor.

Use electric, magnetic, and electromagnetic fields to interact with the object.
- To mix two powders, electrostatically charge one positive and the other negative. Either use fields to direct them, or mix them mechanically and let their acquired fields cause the grains of powder to pair up.

Change from static to movable fields, from unstructured fields to those having structure.
- Early communications used omnidirectional broadcasting. We now use antennas with very detailed structure of the pattern of radiation.

Use fields in conjunction with field-activated (e.g. ferromagnetic) particles.
- Heat a substance containing ferromagnetic material by using varying magnetic field. When the temperature exceeds the Curie point, the material becomes para magnetic and no longer absorbs heat.

Principle 29. Pneumatics and hydraulics
Use gas and liquid parts of an object instead of solid parts (e.g. inflatable, filled with liquids, air cushion, hydrostatic, hydro-reactive).
- Comfortable shoe sole inserts filled with gel.
- Store energy from decelerating a vehicle in a hydraulic system, then use the stored energy to accelerate later.

Principle 30. Flexible shells and thin films
Use flexible shells and thin films instead of three dimensional structures.
- Use inflatable (thin film) structures as winter covers on tennis courts. Isolate the object from the external environment using flexible shells and thin films.
- Float a film of bipolar material (one end hydrophilic, one end hydrophobic) on a reservoir to limit evaporation.

Principle 31. Porous materials
Make an object porous or add porous elements (inserts, coatings, etc.).
- Drill holes in a structure to reduce the weight.

If an object is already porous, use the pores to introduce a useful substance or function.
- Use a porous metal mesh to wick excess solder away from a joint.
- Store hydrogen in the pores of a palladium sponge. (Fuel "tank" for the hydrogen car-much safer than storing hydrogen gas)

Principle 32. Color changes
Change the color of an object or its external environment.
- Use safe lights in a photographic darkroom.

Change the transparency of an object or its external environment.
- Use photolithography to change transparent material to a solid mask for semiconductor processing. Similarly, change mask material from transparent to opaque for silkscreen processing.

Principle 33. Homogeneity
Make objects interacting with a given object of the same material (or material with identical properties).
- Make the container out of the same material as the contents, to reduce chemical reactions.
- Make a diamond cutting tool out of diamonds.

Principle 34. Discarding and recovering
Make portions of an object that have fulfilled their functions go away (discard by dissolving, evaporating, etc.) or modify these directly during operation.
- Use a dissolving capsule for medicine.
- Sprinkle water on cornstarch-based packaging and watch it reduce its volume by more than 1000X!
- Ice structures: use water ice or carbon dioxide (dry ice) to make a template for a rammed earth structure, such as a temporary dam. Fill with earth, then let the ice melt or sublime to leave the final structure.

Conversely, restore consumable parts of an object directly in operation.
- Self-sharpening lawn mower blades.
- Automobile engines that give themselves a "tune up" while running (the ones that say "100,000 miles between tune ups").

Principle 35. Parameter changes
Change an object's physical state (e.g. to a gas, liquid, or solid).
- Freeze the liquid centers of filled candies, then dip in melted chocolate, instead of handling the messy, gooey, hot liquid.
- Transport oxygen or nitrogen or petroleum gas as a liquid, instead of a gas, to reduce volume.

Change the concentration or consistency.
- Liquid hand soap is concentrated and more viscous than bar soap at the point of use, making it easier to dispense in the correct amount and more sanitary when shared by several people.

Change the degree of flexibility.
- Use adjustable dampers to reduce the noise of parts falling into a container by restricting the motion of the walls of the container.
- Vulcanize rubber to change its flexibility and durability.

Change the temperature.
- Raise the temperature above the Curie point to change a ferromagnetic substance to a paramagnetic substance.
- Raise the temperature of food to cook it. (Changes taste, aroma, texture, chemical properties, etc.)
- Lower the temperature of medical specimens to preserve them for later analysis.

Principle 36. Phase transitions
Use phenomena occurring during phase transitions (e.g. volume changes, loss or absorption of heat, etc.).
- Water expands when frozen, unlike most other liquids. Hannibal is reputed

to have used this when marching on Rome a few thousand years ago. Large rocks blocked passages in the Alps. He poured water on them at night. The overnight cold froze the water, and the expansion split the rocks into small pieces which could be pushed aside.

- Heat pumps use the heat of vaporization and heat of condensation of a closed thermodynamic cycle to do useful work.

Principle 37. Thermal expansion
Use thermal expansion (or contraction) of materials.
- Fit a tight joint together by cooling the inner part to contract, heating the outer part to expand, putting the joint together, and returning to equilibrium.

If thermal expansion is being used, use multiple materials with different coefficients of thermal expansion.
- The basic leaf spring thermostat: (two metals with different coefficients of expansion are linked so that it bends one way when warmer than nominal and the opposite way when cooler.)

Principle 38. Strong oxidants
Replace common air with oxygen-enriched air.
- Scuba diving with Nitrox or other non-air mixtures for extended endurance.

Replace enriched air with pure oxygen.
- Cut at a higher temperature using an oxy-acetylene torch.
- Treat wounds in a high pressure oxygen environment to kill anaerobic bacteria and aid healing.

Expose air or oxygen to ionizing radiation.

Use ionized oxygen.
- Ionize air to trap pollutants in an air cleaner.

Replace ozonized (or ionized) oxygen with ozone.
- Speed up chemical reactions by ionizing the gas before use.

Principle 39. Inert atmosphere
Replace a normal environment with an inert one.
- Prevent degradation of a hot metal filament by using an argon atmosphere.

Add neutral parts, or inert additives to an object.
- Increase the volume of powdered detergent by adding inert ingredients. This makes it easier to measure with conventional tools.

Principle 40. Composite materials
Change from uniform to composite (multiple) materials.
- Composite epoxy resin/carbon fiber golf club shafts are lighter, stronger, and more flexible than metal. Same for airplane parts.
- Fiberglass surfboards are lighter and more controllable and easier to form into a variety of shapes than wooden ones.

40 Salamatov, Yuri (edited by Souchkov, Valeri and technical editor, Slocum, Michael), *TRIZ: The Right Solution at the Right Time*, Insytec B.V., The Netherlands, 1999, pp. 222-225.

Appendix 5
The Contradiction Matrix

The contradiction matrix is a 39 x 39 matrix that displays the few inventive principles that apply to resolving any given technical contradiction between two problem parameters. Where you see a "+" in the matrix, this refers to the presence of a physical contradiction, not a technical contradiction. In these cases, you must use the four separation principles (Time, Space, Scale, Condition) to resolve. Where you see a " − " in the matrix, this means that no particular inventive principles are any more likely to aid the resolution of the referenced physical contradiction that any other inventive principles.

Worsening Feature → / Improving Feature ↓	Weight of moving object	Weight of stationary object	Length of moving object	Length of stationary object	Area of moving object	Area of stationary object	Volume of moving object	Volume of stationary object	Speed
	1	2	3	4	5	6	7	8	9
1 Weight of moving object	+	−	15, 8, 29,34	−	29, 17, 38, 34	−	29, 2, 40, 28	−	2, 8, 15, 38
2 Weight of stationary object	−	+	−	10, 1, 29, 35	−	35, 30, 13, 2	−	5, 35, 14, 2	−
3 Length of moving object	8, 15, 29, 34	−	+	−	15, 17, 4	−	7, 17, 4, 35	−	13, 4, 8
4 Length of stationary object	−	35, 28, 40, 29	−	+	−	17, 7, 10, 40	−	35, 8, 2,14	−
5 Area of moving object	2, 17, 29, 4	−	14, 15, 18, 4	−	+	−	7, 14, 17, 4	−	29, 30, 4, 34
6 Area of stationary object	−	30, 2, 14, 18	−	26, 7, 9, 39	−	+	−	−	−
7 Volume of moving object	2, 26, 29, 40	−	1, 7, 4, 35	−	1, 7, 4, 17	−	+	−	29, 4, 38, 34
8 Volume of stationary object	−	35, 10, 19, 14	19, 14	35, 8, 2, 14	−	−	−	+	−
9 Speed	2, 28, 13, 38	−	13, 14, 8	−	29, 30, 34	−	7, 29, 34	−	+
10 Force (Intensity)	8, 1, 37, 18	18, 13, 1, 28	17, 19, 9, 36	28, 10	19, 10, 15	1, 18, 36, 37	15, 9, 12, 37	2, 36, 18, 37	13, 28, 15, 12
11 Stress or pressure	10, 36, 37, 40	13, 29, 10, 18	35, 10, 36	35, 1, 14, 16	10, 15, 36, 28	10, 15, 36, 37	6, 35, 10	35, 24	6, 35, 36
12 Shape	8, 10, 29, 40	15, 10, 26, 3	29, 34, 5, 4	13, 14, 10, 7	5, 34, 4, 10	−	14, 4, 15, 22	7, 2, 35	35, 15, 34, 18
13 Stability of the object's composition	21, 35, 2, 39	26, 39, 1, 40	13, 15, 1, 28	37	2, 11, 13	39	28, 10, 19, 39	34, 28, 35, 40	33, 15, 28, 18
14 Strength	1, 8, 40, 15	40, 26, 27, 1	1, 15, 8, 35	15, 14, 28, 26	3, 34, 40, 29	9, 40, 28	10, 15, 14, 7	9, 14, 17, 15	8, 13, 26, 14
15 Duration of action of moving object	19, 5, 34, 31	−	2, 19, 9	−	3, 17, 19	−	10, 2, 19, 30	−	3, 35, 5
16 Duration of action by stationary object	−	6, 27, 19, 16	−	1, 40, 35	−	−	−	35, 34, 38	−
17 Temperature	36,22, 6, 38	22, 35, 32	15, 19, 9	15, 19, 9	3, 35, 39, 18	35, 38	34, 39, 40, 18	35, 6, 4	2, 28, 36, 30
18 Illumination intensity	19, 1, 32	2, 35, 32	19, 32, 16	−	19, 32, 26	−	2, 13, 10	−	10, 13, 19
19 Use of energy by moving object	12,18, 28,31	−	12, 28	−	15, 19, 25	−	35, 13, 18	−	8, 15, 35
20 Use of energy by stationary object	−	19, 9, 6, 27	−	−	−	−	−	−	−
21 Power	8, 36, 38, 31	19, 26, 17, 27	1, 10, 35, 37	−	19, 38	17, 32, 13, 38	35, 6, 38	30, 6, 25	15, 35, 2
22 Loss of Energy	15, 6, 19, 28	19, 6, 18, 9	7, 2, 6, 13	6, 38, 7	15, 26, 17, 30	17, 7, 30, 18	7, 18, 23	7	16, 35, 38

Worsening Feature → / ↓ Improving Feature	Force (Intensity)	Stress or pressure	Shape	Stability of the object's composition	Strength	Duration of action of moving object	Duration of action of stationary object	Temperature	Illumination intensity
	10	11	12	13	14	15	16	17	18
1 Weight of moving object	8, 10, 18, 37	10, 36, 37, 40	10, 14, 35, 40	1, 35, 19, 39	28, 27, 18, 40	5, 34, 31, 35	–	6, 29, 4, 38	19, 1, 32
2 Weight of stationary object	8, 10, 19, 35	13, 29, 10, 18	13, 10, 29, 14	26, 39, 1, 40	28, 2, 10, 27	–	2, 27, 19, 6	28, 19, 32, 22	19, 32, 35
3 Length of moving object	17, 10, 4	1, 8, 35	1, 8, 10, 29	1, 8, 15, 34	8, 35, 29, 34	19	–	10, 15, 19	32
4 Length of stationary object	28, 10	1, 14, 35	13, 14, 15, 7	39, 37, 35	15, 14, 28, 26	–	1, 40, 35	3, 35, 38, 18	3, 25
5 Area of moving object	19, 30, 35, 2	10, 15, 36, 28	5, 34, 29, 4	11, 2, 13, 39	3, 15, 40, 14	6, 3	–	2, 15, 16	15, 32, 19, 13
6 Area of stationary object	1, 18, 35, 36	10, 15, 36, 37	–	2, 38	40	–	2, 10, 19, 30	35, 39, 38	–
7 Volume of moving object	15, 35, 36, 37	6, 35, 36, 37	1, 15, 29, 4	28, 10, 1, 39	9, 14, 15, 7	6, 35, 4	–	34, 39, 10, 18	2, 13, 10
8 Volume of stationary object	2, 18, 37	24, 35	7, 2, 35	34, 28, 35, 40	9, 14, 17, 15	–	35, 34, 38	35, 6, 4	–
9 Speed	13, 28, 15, 19	6, 18, 38, 40	35, 15, 18, 34	28, 33, 1, 18	8, 3, 26, 14	3, 19, 35, 5	–	28, 30, 36, 2	10, 13, 19
10 Force (Intensity)	+	18, 21, 11	10, 35, 40, 34	35, 10, 21	35, 10, 14, 27	19, 2	–	35, 10, 21	–
11 Stress or pressure	36, 35, 21	+	35, 4, 15, 10	35, 33, 2, 40	9, 18, 3, 40	19, 3, 27	–	35, 39, 19, 2	–
12 Shape	35, 10, 37, 40	34, 15, 10, 14	+	33, 1, 18, 4	30, 14, 10, 40	14, 26, 9, 25	–	22, 14, 19, 32	13, 15, 32
13 Stability of the object's composition	10, 35, 21, 16	2, 35, 40	22, 1, 18, 4	+	17, 9, 15	13, 27, 10, 35	39, 3, 35, 23	35, 1, 32	32, 3, 27, 15
14 Strength	10, 18, 3, 14	10, 3, 18, 40	10, 30, 35, 40	13, 17, 35	+	27, 3, 26	–	30, 10, 40	35, 19
15 Duration of action of moving object	19, 2, 16	19, 3, 27	14, 26, 28, 25	13, 3, 35	27, 3, 10	+	–	19, 35, 39	2, 19, 4, 35
16 Duration of action by stationary object	–	–	–	39, 3, 35, 23	–	–	+	19, 18, 36, 40	–
17 Temperature	35, 10, 3, 21	35, 39, 19, 2	14, 22, 19, 32	1, 35, 32	10, 30, 22, 40	19, 13, 39	19, 18, 36, 40	+	32, 30, 21, 16
18 Illumination intensity	26, 19, 6	–	32, 30	32, 3, 27	35, 19	2, 19, 6	–	32, 35, 19	+
19 Use of energy by moving object	16, 26, 21, 2	23, 14, 25	12, 2, 29	19, 13, 17, 24	5, 19, 9, 35	28, 35, 6, 18	–	19, 24, 3, 14	2, 15, 19
20 Use of energy by stationary object	36, 37	–	–	27, 4, 29, 18	35	–	–	–	19, 2, 35, 32
21 Power	26, 2, 36, 35	22, 10, 35	29, 14, 2, 40	35, 32, 15, 31	26, 10, 28	19, 35, 10, 38	16	2, 14, 17, 25	16, 6, 19
22 Loss of Energy	36, 38	–	–	14, 2, 39, 6	26	–	–	19, 38, 7	1, 13, 32, 15

Worsening Feature → / ↓ Improving Feature	Use of energy by moving object	Use of energy by stationary object	Power	Loss of energy	Loss of substance	Loss of information	Loss of time	Quantity of substance	Reliability
	19	20	21	22	23	24	25	26	27
1 Weight of moving object	35, 12, 34, 31	–	12, 36, 18, 31	6, 2, 34, 19	5, 35, 3, 31	10, 24, 35	10, 35, 20, 28	3, 26, 18, 31	3, 11, 1, 27
2 Weight of stationary object	–	18, 19, 28, 1	15, 19, 18, 22	18, 19, 28, 15	5, 8, 13, 30	10, 15, 35	10, 20, 35, 26	19, 6, 18, 26	10, 28, 8, 3
3 Length of moving object	8, 35, 24	–	1, 35	7, 2, 35, 39	4, 29, 23, 10	1, 24	15, 2, 29	29, 35	10, 14, 29, 40
4 Length of stationary object	–	–	12, 8	6, 28	10, 28, 24, 35	24, 26,	30, 29, 14	–	15, 29, 28
5 Area of moving object	19, 32	–	19, 10, 32, 18	15, 17, 30, 26	10, 35, 2, 39	30, 26	26, 4	29, 30, 6, 13	29, 9
6 Area of stationary object	–	–	17, 32	17, 7, 30	10, 14, 18, 39	30, 16	10, 35, 4, 18	2, 18, 40, 4	32, 35, 40, 4
7 Volume of moving object	35	–	35, 6, 13, 18	7, 15, 13, 16	36, 39, 34, 10	2, 22	2, 6, 34, 10	29, 30, 7	14, 1, 40, 11
8 Volume of stationary object	–	–	30, 6	–	10, 39, 35, 34	–	35, 16, 32 18	35, 3	2, 35, 16
9 Speed	8, 15, 35, 38	–	19, 35, 38, 2	14, 20, 19, 35	10, 13, 28, 38	13, 26	–	10, 19, 29, 38	11, 35, 27, 28
10 Force (Intensity)	19, 17, 10	1, 16, 36, 37	19, 35, 18, 37	14, 15	8, 35, 40, 5	–	10, 37, 36	14, 29, 18, 36	3, 35, 13, 21
11 Stress or pressure	14, 24, 10, 37	–	10, 35, 14	2, 36, 25	10, 36, 3, 37	–	37, 36, 4	10, 14, 36	10, 13, 19, 35
12 Shape	2, 6, 34, 14	–	4, 6, 2	14	35, 29, 3, 5	–	14, 10, 34, 17	36, 22	10, 40, 16
13 Stability of the object's composition	13, 19	27, 4, 29, 18	32, 35, 27, 31	14, 2, 39, 6	2, 14, 30, 40	–	35, 27	15, 32, 35	–
14 Strength	19, 35, 10	35	10, 26, 35, 28	35	35, 28, 31, 40	–	29, 3, 28, 10	29, 10, 27	11, 3
15 Duration of action of moving object	28, 6, 35, 18	–	19, 10, 35, 38	–	28, 27, 3, 18	10	20, 10, 28, 18	3, 35, 10, 40	11, 2, 13
16 Duration of action by stationary object	–	–	16	–	27, 16, 18, 38	10	28, 20, 10, 16	3, 35, 31	34, 27, 6, 40
17 Temperature	19, 15, 3, 17	–	2, 14, 17, 25	21, 17, 35, 38	21, 36, 29, 31	–	35, 28, 21, 18	3, 17, 30, 39	19, 35, 3, 10
18 Illumination intensity	32, 1, 19	32, 35, 1, 15	32	13, 16, 1, 6	13, 1	1, 6	19, 1, 26, 17	1, 19	–
19 Use of energy by moving object	+	·	6, 19, 37, 18	12, 22, 15, 24	35, 24, 18, 5	–	35, 38, 19, 18	34, 23, 16, 18	19, 21, 11, 27
20 Use of energy by stationary object	–	+	–	–	28, 27, 18, 31	–	–	3, 35, 31	10, 36, 23
21 Power	16, 6, 19, 37	–	+	10, 35, 38	28, 27, 18, 38	10, 19	35, 20, 10, 6	4, 34, 19	19, 24, 26, 31
22 Loss of Energy	–	–	3, 38	+	35, 27, 2, 37	19, 10	10, 18, 32, 7	7, 18, 25	11, 10, 35

Worsening Feature → / Improving Feature ↓	Measurement accuracy	Manufacturing precision	Object-affected harmful factors	Object-generated harmful factors	Ease of manufacture	Ease of operation	Ease of repair	Adaptability or versatility	Device complexity
	28	29	30	31	32	33	34	35	36
1 Weight of moving object	28, 27, 35, 26	28, 35, 26, 18	22, 21, 18, 27	22, 35, 31, 39	27, 28, 1, 36	35, 3, 2, 24	2, 27, 28, 11	29, 5, 15, 8	26, 30, 36, 34
2 Weight of stationary object	18, 26, 28	10, 1, 35, 17	2, 19, 22, 37	35, 22, 1, 39	28, 1, 9	6, 13, 1, 32	2, 27, 28, 11	19, 15, 29	1, 10, 26, 39
3 Length of moving object	28, 32, 4	10, 28, 29, 37	1, 15, 17, 24	17, 15	1, 29, 17	15, 29, 35, 4	1, 28, 10	14, 15, 1, 16	1, 19, 26, 24
4 Length of stationary object	32, 28, 3	2, 32, 10	1, 18	–	15, 17, 27	2, 25	3	1, 35	1, 26
5 Area of moving object	26, 28, 32, 3	2, 32	22, 33, 28, 1	17, 2, 18, 39	13, 1, 26, 24	15, 17, 13, 16	15, 13, 10, 1	15, 30	14, 1, 13
6 Area of stationary object	26, 28, 32, 3	2, 29, 18, 36	27, 2, 39, 35	22, 1, 40	40, 16	16, 4	16	15, 16	1, 18, 36
7 Volume of moving object	25, 26, 28	25, 28, 2, 16	22, 21, 27, 35	17, 2, 40, 1	29, 1, 40	15, 13, 30, 12	10	15, 29	26, 1
8 Volume of stationary object	–	35, 10, 25	34, 39, 19, 27	30, 18, 35, 4	35	–	1	–	1, 31
9 Speed	28, 32, 1, 24	10, 28, 32, 25	1, 28, 35, 23	2, 24, 35, 21	35, 13, 8, 1	32, 28, 13, 12	34, 2, 28, 27	15, 10, 26	10, 28, 4, 34
10 Force (Intensity)	35, 10, 23, 24	28, 29, 37, 36	1, 35, 40, 18	13, 3, 36, 24	15, 37, 18, 1	1, 28, 3, 25	15, 1, 11	15, 17, 18, 20	26, 35, 10, 18
11 Stress or pressure	6, 28, 25	3, 35	22, 2, 37	2, 33, 27, 18	1, 35, 16	11	2	35	19, 1, 35
12 Shape	28, 32, 1	32, 30, 40	22, 1, 2, 35	35, 1	1, 32, 17, 28	32, 15, 26	2, 13, 1	1, 15, 29	16, 29, 1, 28
13 Stability of the object's composition	13	18	35, 24, 30, 18	35, 40, 27, 39	35, 19	32, 35, 30	2, 35, 10, 16	35, 30, 34, 2	2, 35, 22, 26
14 Strength	3, 27, 16	3, 27	18, 35, 37, 1	15, 35, 22, 2	11, 3, 10, 32	32, 40, 28, 2	27, 11, 3	15, 3, 32	2, 13, 28
15 Duration of action of moving object	3	3, 27, 16, 40	22, 15, 33, 28	21, 39, 16, 22	27, 1, 4	12, 27	29, 10, 27	1, 35, 13	10, 4, 29, 15
16 Duration of action by stationary object	10, 26, 24	–	17, 1, 40, 33	22	35, 10	1	1	2	–
17 Temperature	32, 19, 24	24	22, 33, 35, 2	22, 35, 2, 24	26, 27	26, 27	4, 10, 16	2, 18, 27	2, 17, 16
18 Illumination intensity	11, 15, 32	3, 32	15, 19	35, 19, 32, 39	19, 35, 28, 26	28, 26, 19	15, 17, 13, 16	15, 1, 19	6, 32, 13
19 Use of energy by moving object	3, 1, 32	–	1, 35, 6, 27	2, 35, 6	28, 26, 30	19, 35	1, 15, 17, 28	15, 17, 13, 16	2, 29, 27, 28
20 Use of energy by stationary object	–	–	10, 2, 22, 37	19, 22, 18	1, 4	–	–	–	–
21 Power	32, 15, 2	32, 2	19, 22, 31, 2	2, 35, 18	26, 10, 34	26, 35, 10	35, 2, 10, 34	19, 17, 34	20, 19, 30, 34
22 Loss of Energy	32	–	21, 22, 35, 2	21, 35, 2, 22	–	35, 32, 1	2, 19	–	7, 23

Worsening Feature → / Improving Feature ↓	Difficulty of detecting and measuring	Extent of automation	Productivity
	37	38	39
1	Weight of moving object	28, 29, 26, 32	26, 35 18, 19	35, 3, 24, 37
2	Weight of stationary object	25, 28, 17, 15	2, 26, 35	1, 28, 15, 35
3	Length of moving object	35, 1, 26, 24	17, 24, 26, 16	14, 4, 28, 29
4	Length of stationary object	26	–	30, 14, 7, 26
5	Area of moving object	2, 36, 26, 18	14, 30, 28, 23	10, 26, 34, 2
6	Area of stationary object	2, 35, 30, 18	23	10, 15, 17, 7
7	Volume of moving object	29, 26, 4	35, 34, 16, 24	10, 6, 2, 34
8	Volume of stationary object	2, 17, 26	–	35, 37, 10, 2
9	Speed	3, 34, 27, 16	10, 18	–
10	Force (Intensity)	36, 37, 10, 19	2, 35	3, 28, 35, 37
11	Stress or pressure	2, 36, 37	35, 24	10, 14, 35, 37
12	Shape	15, 13, 39	15, 1, 32	17, 26, 34, 10
13	Stability of the object's composition	35, 22, 39, 23	1, 8, 35	23, 35, 40, 3
14	Strength	27, 3, 15, 40	15	29, 35, 10, 14
15	Duration of action of moving object	19, 29, 39, 35	6, 10	35, 17, 14, 19
16	Duration of action by stationary object	25, 34, 6, 35	1	20, 10, 16, 38
17	Temperature	3, 27, 35, 31	26, 2, 19, 16	15, 28, 35
18	Illumination intensity	32, 15	2, 26, 10	2, 25, 16
19	Use of energy by moving object	35, 38	32, 2	12, 28, 35
20	Use of energy by stationary object	19, 35, 16, 25	–	1, 6
21	Power	19, 35, 16	28, 2, 17	28, 35, 34
22	Loss of energy	35, 3, 15, 23	2	28, 10, 29, 35

Worsening Feature → / Improving Feature ↓	Weight of moving object	Weight of stationary object	Length of moving object	Length of stationary object	Area of moving object	Area of stationary object	Volume of moving object	Volume of stationary object	Speed
	1	2	3	4	5	6	7	8	9
23 Loss of substance	35, 6, 23, 40	35, 6, 22, 32	14, 29, 10, 39	10, 28, 24	35, 2, 10, 31	10, 18, 39, 31	1, 29, 30, 36	3, 39, 18, 31	10, 13, 28, 38
24 Loss of information	10, 24, 35	10, 35, 5	1, 26	26	30, 26	30, 16	–	2, 22	26, 32
25 Loss of time	10, 20, 37, 35	10, 20, 26, 5	15, 2, 29	30, 24, 14, 5	26, 4, 5, 16	10, 35, 17, 4	2, 5, 34, 10	35, 16, 32, 18	–
26 Quantity of substance/the matter	35, 6, 18, 31	27, 26, 18, 35	29, 14, 35, 18	–	15, 14, 29	2, 18, 40, 4	15, 20, 29	–	35, 29, 34, 28
27 Reliability	3, 8, 10, 40	3, 10, 8, 28	15, 9, 14, 4	15, 29, 28, 11	17, 10, 14, 16	32, 35, 40, 4	3, 10, 14, 24	2, 35, 24	21, 35, 11, 28
28 Measurement accuracy	32, 35, 26, 28	28, 35, 25, 26	28, 26, 5, 16	32, 28, 3, 16	26, 28, 32, 3	26, 28, 32, 3	32, 13, 6	–	28, 13, 32, 24
29 Manufacturing precision	28, 32, 13, 18	28, 35, 27, 9	10, 28, 29, 37	2, 32, 10	28, 33, 29, 32	2, 29, 18, 36	32, 38, 2	25, 10, 35	10, 28, 32
30 Object-affected harmful factors	22, 21, 27, 39	2, 22, 13, 24	17, 1, 39, 4	1, 18	22, 1, 33, 28	27, 2, 39, 35	22, 23, 37, 35	34, 39, 19, 27	21, 22, 35, 28
31 Object-generated harmful factors	19, 22, 15, 39	35, 22, 1, 39	17, 15, 16, 22	–	17, 2, 18, 39	22, 1, 40	17, 2, 40	30, 18, 35, 4	35, 28, 3, 23
32 Ease of manufacture	28, 29, 15, 16	1, 27, 36, 13	1, 29, 13, 17	15, 17, 27	13, 1, 26, 12	16, 40	13, 29, 1, 40	35	35, 13, 8, 1
33 Ease of operation	25, 2, 13, 15	6, 13, 1, 25	1, 17, 13, 12	–	1, 17, 13, 16	18, 16, 15, 39	1, 16, 35, 15	4, 18, 39, 31	18, 13, 34
34 Ease of repair	2, 27, 35, 11	2, 27, 35, 11	1, 28, 10, 25	3, 18, 31	15, 13, 32	16, 25	25, 2, 35, 11	1	34, 9
35 Adaptability or versatility	1, 6, 15, 8	19, 15, 29, 16	35, 1, 29, 2	1, 35, 16	35, 30, 29, 7	15, 16	15, 35, 29	–	35, 10, 14
36 Device complexity	26, 30, 34, 36	2, 26, 35, 39	1, 19, 26, 24	26	14, 1, 13, 16	6, 36	34, 26, 6	1, 16	34, 10, 28
37 Difficulty of detecting and measuring	27, 26, 28, 13	6, 13, 28, 1	16, 17, 26, 24	26	2, 13, 18, 17	2, 39, 30, 16	29, 1, 4, 16	2, 18, 26, 31	3, 4, 16, 35
38 Extent of automation	28, 26, 18, 35	28, 26, 35, 10	14, 13, 17, 28	23	17, 14, 13	–	35, 13, 16	–	28, 10
39 Productivity	35, 26, 24, 37	28, 27, 15, 3	18, 4, 28, 38	30, 7, 14, 26	10, 26, 34, 31	10, 35, 17, 7	2, 6, 34, 10	35, 37, 10, 2	–

Worsening Feature ⇒ Improving Feature ⇓	Force (Intensity)	Stress or pressure	Shape	Stability of the object's composition	Strength	Duration of action of moving object	Duration of action of object stationary	Temperature	Illumination intensity
	10	11	12	13	14	15	16	17	18
23 Loss of substance	14, 15, 18, 40	3, 36, 37, 10	29, 35, 3, 5	2, 14, 30, 40	35, 28, 31, 40	28, 27, 3, 18	27, 16, 18, 38	21, 36, 39, 31	1, 6, 13
24 Loss of information	–	–	–	–	–	10	10	–	19
25 Loss of time	10, 37, 36,5	37, 36,4	4, 10, 34, 17	35, 3, 22, 5	29, 3, 28, 18	20, 10, 28, 18	28, 20, 10, 16	35, 29, 21, 18	1, 19, 26, 17
26 Quantity of substance/the matter	35, 14, 3	10, 36, 14, 3	35, 14	15, 2, 17, 40	14, 35, 34, 10	3, 35, 10, 40	3, 35, 31	3, 17, 39	–
27 Reliability	8, 28, 10, 3	10, 24, 35, 19	35, 1, 16, 11	–	11, 28	2, 35, 3, 25	34, 27, 6, 40	3, 35, 10	11, 32, 13
28 Measurement accuracy	32, 2	6, 28, 32	6, 28, 32	32, 35, 13	28, 6, 32	28, 6, 32	10, 26, 24	6, 19, 28, 24	6, 1, 32
29 Manufacturing precision	28, 19, 34, 36	3, 35	32, 30, 40	30, 18	3, 27	3, 27, 40	–	19, 26	3, 32
30 Object-affected harmful factors	13, 35, 39, 18	22, 2, 37	22, 1, 3, 35	35, 24, 30, 18	18, 35, 37, 1	22, 15, 33, 28	17, 1, 40, 33	22, 33, 35, 2	1, 19, 32, 13
31 Object-generated harmful factors	35, 28, 1, 40	2, 33, 27, 18	35, 1	35, 40, 27, 39	15, 35, 22, 2	15, 22, 33, 31	21, 39, 16, 22	22, 35, 2, 24	19, 24, 39, 32
32 Ease of manufacture	35, 12	35, 19, 1, 37	1, 28, 13, 27	11, 13, 1	1, 3, 10, 32	27, 1, 4	35, 16	27, 26, 18	28, 24, 27, 1
33 Ease of operation	28, 13, 35	2, 32, 12	15, 34, 29, 28	32, 35, 30	32, 40, 3, 28	29, 3, 8, 25	1, 16, 25	26, 27, 13	13, 17, 1, 24
34 Ease of repair	1, 11, 10	13	1, 13, 2, 4	2, 35	11, 1, 2, 9	11, 29, 28, 27	1	4, 10	15, 1, 13
35 Adaptability or versatility	15, 17, 20	35, 16	15, 37, 1, 8	35, 30, 14	35, 3, 32, 6	13, 1, 35	2, 16	27, 2, 3, 35	6, 22, 26, 1
36 Device complexity	26, 16	19, 1, 35	29, 13, 28, 15	2, 22, 17, 19	2, 13, 28	10, 4, 28, 15	–	2, 17, 13	24, 17, 13
37 Difficulty of detecting and measuring	36, 28, 40, 19	35, 36, 37, 32	27, 13, 1, 39	11, 22, 39, 30	27, 3, 15, 28	19, 29, 39, 25	25, 34, 6, 35	3, 27, 35, 16	2, 24, 26
38 Extent of automation	2, 35	13, 35	15, 32, 1, 13	18, 1	25, 13	6, 9	–	26, 2, 19	8, 32, 19
39 Productivity	28, 15, 10, 36	10, 37, 14	14, 10, 34, 40	35, 3, 22, 39	29, 28, 10, 18	35, 10, 2, 18	20, 10, 16, 38	35, 21, 28, 10	26, 17, 19, 1

Improving Feature \ Worsening Feature		Use of energy by moving object	Use of energy by stationary object	Power	Loss of energy	Loss of substance	Loss of information	Loss of time	Quantity of substance	Reliability
		19	20	21	22	23	24	25	26	27
23	Loss of substance	35, 18, 24, 5	28, 27, 12, 31	28, 27, 18, 38	35, 27, 2, 31	+	−	15, 18, 35, 10	6, 3, 10, 24	10, 29, 39, 35
24	Loss of information	−	−	10, 19	19, 10	−	+	24, 26, 28, 32	24, 28, 35	10, 28, 23
25	Loss of time	35, 38, 19, 18	1	35, 20, 10, 6	10, 5, 18, 32	35, 18, 10, 39	24, 26, 28, 32	+	35, 38, 18, 16	10, 30, 4
26	Quantity of substance/the matter	34, 29, 16, 18	3, 35, 31	35	7, 18, 25	6, 3, 10, 24	24, 28, 35	35, 38, 18, 16	+	18, 3, 28, 40
27	Reliability	21, 11, 27, 19	36, 23	21, 11, 26, 31	10, 11, 35	10, 35, 29, 39	10, 28	10, 30, 4	21, 28, 40, 3	+
28	Measurement accuracy	3, 6, 32	−	3, 6, 32	26, 32, 27	10, 16, 31, 28	−	24, 34, 28, 32	2, 6, 32	5, 11, 1, 23
29	Manufacturing precision	32, 2	−	32, 2	13, 32, 2	35, 31, 10, 24	−	32, 26, 28, 18	32, 30	11, 32, 1
30	Object-affected harmful factors	1, 24, 6, 27	10, 2, 22, 37	19, 22, 31, 2	21, 22, 35, 2	33, 22, 19, 40	22, 10, 2	35, 18, 34	35, 33, 29, 31	27, 24, 2, 40
31	Object-generated harmful factors	2, 35, 6	19, 22, 18	2, 35, 18	21, 35, 2, 22	10, 1, 34	10, 21, 29	1, 22	3, 24, 39, 1	24, 2, 40, 39
32	Ease of manufacture	28, 26, 27, 1	1, 4	27, 1, 12, 24	19, 35	15, 34, 33	32, 24, 18, 16	35, 28, 34, 4	35, 23, 1, 24	−
33	Ease of operation	1, 13, 24	−	35, 34, 2, 10	2, 19, 13	28, 32, 2, 24	4, 10, 27, 22	4, 28, 10, 34	12, 35	17, 27, 8, 40
34	Ease of repair	15, 1, 28, 16	−	15, 10, 32, 2	15, 1, 32, 19	2, 35, 34, 27	−	32, 1, 10, 25	2, 28, 10, 25	11, 10, 1, 16
35	Adaptability or versatility	19, 35, 29, 13	−	19, 1, 29	18, 15, 1	15, 10, 2, 13	−	35, 28	3, 35, 15	35, 13, 8, 24
36	Device complexity	27, 2, 29, 28	−	20, 19, 30, 34	10, 35, 13, 2	35, 10, 28, 29	−	6, 29	13, 3, 27, 10	13, 35, 1
37	Difficulty of detecting and measuring	35, 38	19, 35, 16	19, 1, 16, 10	35, 3, 15, 19	1, 18, 10, 24	35, 33, 27, 22	18, 28, 32, 9	3, 27, 29, 18	27, 40, 28, 8
38	Extent of automation	2, 32, 13	−	28, 2, 27	23, 28	35, 10, 18, 5	35, 33	24, 28, 35, 30	35, 13	11, 27, 32
39	Productivity	35, 10, 38, 19	1	35, 20, 10	28, 10, 29, 35	28, 10, 35, 23	13, 15, 23	−	35, 38	1, 35, 10, 38

Worsening Feature ⟹ / Improving Feature ⬇	Measurement accuracy	Manufacturing precision	Object-affected harmful factors	Object-generated harmful factors	Ease of manufacture	Ease of operation	Ease of repair	Adaptability or versatility	Device complexity
	28	29	30	31	32	33	34	35	36
23 Loss of substance	16, 34, 31, 28	35, 10, 24, 31	33, 22, 30, 40	10, 1, 34, 29	15, 34, 33	32, 28, 2, 24	2, 35, 34, 27	15, 10, 2	35, 10, 28, 24
24 Loss of information	–	–	22, 10, 1	10, 21, 22	32	27, 22	–	–	–
25 Loss of time	24, 34, 28, 32	24, 26, 28, 18	35, 18, 34	35, 22, 18, 39	35, 28, 34, 4	4, 28, 10, 34	32, 1, 10	35, 28	6, 29
26 Quantity of substance/the matter	13, 2, 28	33, 30	35, 33, 29, 31	3, 35, 40, 39	29, 1, 35, 27	35, 29, 25, 10	2, 32, 10, 25	15, 3, 29	3, 13, 27, 10
27 Reliability	32, 3, 11, 23	11, 32, 1	27, 35, 2, 40	35, 2, 40, 26	–	27, 17, 40	1, 11	13, 35, 8, 24	13, 35, 1
28 Measurement accuracy	+	–	28, 24, 22, 26	3, 33, 39, 10	6, 35, 25, 18	1, 13, 17, 34	1, 32, 13, 11	13, 35, 2	27, 35, 10, 34
29 Manufacturing precision	–	+	26, 28, 10, 36	4, 17, 34, 26	–	1, 32, 35, 23	25, 10	–	26, 2, 18
30 Object-affected harmful factors	28, 33, 23, 26	26, 28, 10, 18	+	–	24, 35, 2	2, 25, 28, 39	35, 10, 2	35, 11, 22, 31	22, 19, 29, 40
31 Object-generated harmful factors	3, 33, 26	4, 17, 34, 26	–	+	–	–	–	–	19, 1, 31
32 Ease of manufacture	1, 35, 12, 18	–	24, 2	–	+	2, 5, 13, 16	35, 1, 11, 9	2, 13, 15	27, 26, 1
33 Ease of operation	25, 13, 2, 34	1, 32, 35, 23	2, 25, 28, 39	–	2, 5, 12	+	12, 26, 1, 32	15, 34, 1, 16	32, 26, 12, 17
34 Ease of repair	10, 2, 13	25, 10	35, 10, 2, 16	–	1, 35, 11, 10	1, 12, 26, 15	+	7, 1, 4, 16	35, 1, 13, 11
35 Adaptability or versatility	35, 5, 1, 10	–	35, 11, 32, 31	–	1, 13, 31	15, 34, 1, 16	1, 16, 7, 4	+	15, 29, 37, 28
36 Device complexity	2, 26, 10, 34	26, 24, 32	22, 19, 29, 40	19, 1	27, 26, 1, 13	27, 9, 26, 24	1, 13	29, 15, 28, 37	+
37 Difficulty of detecting and measuring	26, 24, 32, 28	–	22, 19, 29, 28	2, 21	5, 28, 11, 29	2, 5	12, 26	1, 15	15, 10, 37, 28
38 Extent of automation	28, 26, 10, 34	28, 26, 18, 23	2, 33	2	1, 26, 13	1, 12, 34, 3	1, 35, 13	27, 4, 1, 35	15, 24, 10
39 Productivity	1, 10, 34, 28	18, 10, 32, 1	22, 35, 13, 24	35, 22, 18, 39	35, 28, 2, 24	1, 28, 7, 19	1, 32, 10, 25	1, 35, 28, 37	12, 17, 28, 24

		Difficulty of detecting and measuring	Extent of automation	Productivity
		37	38	39
23	Loss of substance	35, 18, 10, 13	35, 10, 18	28, 35, 10, 23
24	Loss of information	35, 33	35	13, 23, 15
25	Loss of time	18, 28, 32, 10	24, 28, 35, 30	–
26	Quantity of substance/the matter	3, 27, 29, 18	8, 35	13, 29, 3, 27
27	Reliability	27, 40, 28	11, 13, 27	1, 35, 29, 38
28	Measurement accuracy	26, 24, 32, 28	28, 2, 10, 34	10, 34, 28, 32
29	Manufacturing precision	–	26, 28, 18, 23	10, 18, 32, 39
30	Object-affected harmful factors	22, 19, 29, 40	33, 3, 34	22, 35, 13, 24
31	Object-generated harmful factors	2, 21, 27, 1	2	22, 35, 18, 39
32	Ease of manufacture	6, 28, 11, 1	8, 28, 1	35, 1, 10, 28
33	Ease of operation	–	1, 34, 12, 3	15, 1, 28
34	Ease of repair	–	34, 35, 7, 13	1, 32, 10
35	Adaptability or versatility	1	27, 34, 35	35, 28, 6, 37
36	Device complexity	15, 10, 37, 28	15, 1, 24	12, 17, 28
37	Difficulty of detecting and measuring	+	34, 21	35, 18
38	Extent of automation	34, 27, 25	+	5, 12, 35, 26
39	Productivity	35, 18, 27, 2	5, 12, 35, 26	+

Worsening Feature ⇨

Improving Feature ⬇

Index